TED MATTSON

For my grandsons Henry and Kyle

Also by Ted Mattson:

The Eye of the Rainbow

Adventures of the Iditarod Air Force

About the Photographs

Special thanks to Jimmy Lira of sdtunaboats@cox.net for graciously providing the book's cover photograph.

The photo of the author on the back page was taken by Whit Deschner.

Labor Day Hunkin took the photo on page 24.

All other photos are by the author.

The Tuna Boys
©2023 Ted Mattson

print ISBN: 978-1-66788-157-7
ebook ISBN: 978-1-66788-158-4

CONTENTS

ACKNOWLEDGEMENTS

Where to start? So many people, so many favors, but certainly this project wouldn't have taken legs without the help of Whit Deschner. Whit has been encouraging me for more years than I care to count to not let this adventure of my life die. "At least get it down on paper for your grandsons, Ted." And while that was my intention all along, the journal stayed closed, gathering dust for way too many years. Thank you, Whit, for never giving up on me.

Mathew Stevenson was more than gracious to welcome me into his home office, where I could sit at his side while he utilized his super color printer to turn my thirty-eight-year old photos into a potential book cover as well as possible photos for the book's interior. I've lost track of how many visits I made to his basement office where he publishes a monthly newsletter for our local veterans. Unfortunately, Bookbaby.com rejected all of my potential cover photos because they needed more pixels. "Could I take them again with a better camera?" Since I took the photos thirty-eight years ago, the answer was obvious. Regardless, Matt, I can't thank you enough for your efforts.

Roman Paluta, who spends summers at his family home down the road from us, volunteered to proofread, utilizing his longtime advertising skills to the fullest. And for that I am sincerely thankful. I should add that having an author/editor (me) who commonly transposes letters as well as numbers probably was a poor choice to correct the mistakes Roman so patiently pointed out. No matter, responsibility for the final outcome rests with me.

To Nancy Danner goes another big thank you. I prevailed upon Nancy to read the earliest versions of the manuscript as a "disinterested" reader, mistakes and all. Her questions about things I thought were straightforward about seine boats, commercial fishing in general, and flying helicopters are hopefully now not foreign languages to anyone who might open the pages to see what the book's about.

Other early readers were: Steve Corbeille, Bob Mielke, and John Zimmerman, whose enthusiasm pushed me to keep going and I thank you all for that.

Thanks to David Botich for help with helicopter maintenance technicalities.

To Mike Croft, who has made the thirteen-mile drive to our place every Wednesday evening for at least five years, I am indebted as well. We enjoy a cup of tea and maybe a cookie or two while we talk about the books we recently exchanged or are currently reading as well as solving most of the world's problems. Mike read only one page of the manuscript. "I hear your voice loud and clear, Ted. Put me down for a copy." Well Mike, it's here.

Microsoft Word and I don't cross paths very often but Linda Waller and Tom Doering helped make my interaction with it bearable. Linda was visiting from Alaska with limited time but the book now has a map because of her. Tom lives a few miles away but came and sat beside me at my computer whenever I got stuck. Oh, what I'd give to have the computer skills each of them has! I can't thank you both enough.

Andy White was the chief engineer aboard the Pacific Princess and is the only person I've remotely kept in contact with. I asked Andy to identify countless photos of the Samoan and Peruvian crew members who were also on the trip we shared together. And while Andy put names on many of the photos I sent his way, only two were listed in my journal: Andy and Filipo. Andy had been on so many other tuna boats in his career, names came to him but not the names for the guys on our trip. Note to Ted: "Always write people's names on the back of all photos."

I can't leave out the identical twins, Cindy Plaza, my bride of fifteen years, and Phyllis Mulligan, who was visiting when all this was taking place. Phyllis took countless potential author photos in all possible lighting scenarios only to have them vetoed by Whit Deschner. His keen eye for evaluating anything involving photos is amazing. But Phyllis, how would we have known otherwise? Your efforts were exemplary and I thank you.

And finally, to Cindy Plaza who has taken every one of my harebrained ideas in stride. She was no different this time around as she watched the first book she'd ever seen being written slowly come together. Piles of papers strewn everywhere. Questions of, "How does this sound?" And a few minutes later, "Okay, now listen to it again." These were daily occurrences for over a year and half but she was always there. Thank you, Cindy, because you made the book better.

FOREWORD
(WITH MAP)

What I'm about to introduce you to is based on events in my life thirty-eight years ago. And while I included a chapter about these events in my earlier book *The Eye of the Rainbow,* the events were not detailed. The daily journal I kept at the time and hung on to all these years has been invaluable in refreshing my memory. I was amazed at how much I "remembered" incorrectly. Some events stand out clearly but the majority of journal entries were mundane happenings, so I picked and chose what to include here. The journal entries are clearly written in **bold type** and include the day and date and usually some indication of our direction of travel or what landmark we might have happened to be near at the time. Some were written shortly after they happened but most are from how I remembered what happened when I finally got around to recording in my journal when I crawled into bed at night. All the boats mentioned in the book are emphasized in ***bold italics.***

It also became apparent that some sort of a map was necessary to give the reader a sense of where all this was taking place. The map is certainly not to scale but it does depict how big the area was in which we fished. As an example, when we finally got the word to head home, we were 400 miles south of Guam and were looking at 3,000 miles of travel to get back to where we started. The Pacific Ocean isn't called the largest ocean in the world for nothing.

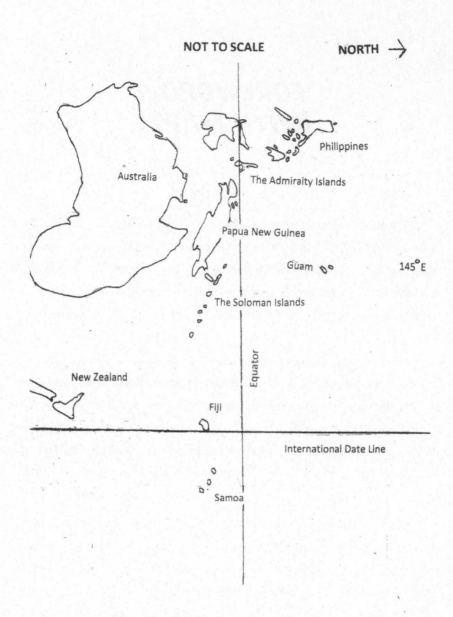

INTRODUCTION

The Tuna Boys is about the time I flew a helicopter off a big super seiner in the Western Pacific as the tuna spotter pilot. All these years later, I'm still telling stories about the time I went to sea for over three months south of the equator as a means of getting away from another Alaskan winter. And while I commercially fished for Alaska's salmon in the Bering Sea, I'd never really been "out to sea." After my divorce and move to Alaska, I learned very quickly there was nothing you could do in Alaska during December, January, or February that couldn't be done better somewhere else and I was always curiously looking for something to do during those months. The more exciting, the better.

"Ted, you don't do a darn thing in the winter. Why don't you come down to San Diego and fly the helicopter off one of those tuna boats in the harbor?" It was Gene Golles giving me another razing from his San Diego living room. I'd stopped in to say hello near the end of a winter of traveling throughout the southwestern U.S. Gene was one of my oldest fishing friends from Alaska's Bristol Bay. We went way back to when we fished in outboard equipped skiffs. We had both come a long way over the years. He now had his wife Lou up there with him, so I'd known them both a long time and felt comfortable staying with them a few days when they insisted. I was about to head back to Alaska when he told me about the helicopters and the tuna boats.

On my way out of town, I stopped along the waterfront in downtown San Diego and there they were. Probably the most beautiful and certainly the longest seiners I'd ever imagined. Years before, I fell in love with the sleek forty-two-foot Kodiak Deltas that fished the herring runs in Togiak. But these were 220 footers. Eleven-hundred-ton-capacity super seiners. Sleek giants of the sea. True ocean-going vessels that would stay out in any kind of weather until their fifteen enormous fish holds were stuffed with the frozen tuna that helped feed a large portion of the world. But high overhead on the uppermost part of the flying bridge, nearly three stories above me, was the most beautiful ship of all—the helicopter. I'd been in love with choppers longer than boats, except, of course, for my *Old Town* canoe. Helicopters did the impossible—ten thousand moving parts all trying to come apart at the same time, and yet, it flew. But more than that, it hovered. My T-shirt said it all: "**To fly may be heavenly but to hover is divine.**" I hadn't been around helicopters much since I started commercial fishing, but the desire was always there.

Just the thought of spending a warm winter at sea with a helicopter under my command had my heart pounding. The kind of adventure I craved.

I could feel my senses shifting into search and secure mode. I'd learned years before that what you know isn't nearly as important as who you know, and I set about right then getting to know someone who knew something about helicopters and tuna boats. Fortunately, I've never had any trouble talking to people and soon found my way aboard *The Conquistador*, chatting with anyone who would talk. The fact that I was a helicopter jockey as well as an Alaskan fisherman certainly made it easier. Soon I was being shown around the engine room and the galley and even the captain's quarters. When we climbed to the topmost deck to check out the bird, I was hooked.

But I was also on my way back to Alaska. All I could really do was jot down a few names of possible contacts and do whatever I could once I got North.

CHAPTER 1

GETTING STARTED

Tuesday, December 27, 1984
(Palmer, Alaska)

A year after the call from Gene, I was still trying to get on a tuna boat. I knew now I needed to be down where the action was. I would give myself thirty days to get a job or give it up. I bought an airline ticket to Seattle and packed my bags.

Sometime prior to Christmas, I got the urge to stop in at Wilbur's Flight Service in Anchorage and get some flying time. I bought a couple of hours in their Bell 47, the workhorse of piston-driven choppers that have been around since the Korean War. If you've ever watched MASH, you've seen the early version of the Bell 47. They've been upgraded a lot since then. Surprisingly, it went pretty well. Not unlike riding a bicycle because it did come back. I actually did a couple of run-on autorotations on a frozen lake after the instructor demonstrated one to me. An autorotation is where you land the helicopter by disengaging the rotor blades from the power of the helicopter's engine and then use the inertia of the spinning blades to cushion your landing. The trick is to not use up all the inertia in the blades before the helicopter is safely down where you want it to land.

In Seattle, I retrieved my old Ford camping van I'd stored at Magnar Warness', another Bristol Bay fishing friend, where I'd spent the night. Next day, I was on my way to Dana Point in Southern California where my cousin

Dahlin and her four kids lived. With my van, I had a place to sleep as well as a base of operations. Lots of tuna activity along the coastline and I planned to explore every bit of it I could find.

Friday, January 11, 1985
(Dana Point, CA)

Nearly two weeks and 3,000 miles of driving up and down the coast behind me, I was getting antsy. Like treading water with no place to go—just waiting for something to happen. The tuna business is tough but there was something inside me that wanted me to get in. Maybe just the challenge. I plugged along some more and kept stumbling onto leads and knew if I had enough perseverance, it would come together eventually. Whether that is this year or not remained to be seen at this point. I evidently needed to meet Bud Levit in San Diego. He is supposed to be the man that all tuna boats look to for pilots.

Wednesday, January 16, 1985
(At Golles' in San Diego)

It was very pleasant walking around the Golles' back yard this morning. Birds singing, warm smell of spring in the air, plants flourishing, lemons for the picking. Really homey and nice.

Also, nice to catch up on some of my mail. Although my phone bill wasn't so nice.

Friday, January 18, 1985
(Bud Levit's office, Brown Field Municipal A/P)

Bingo! Finally at the right place at the right time. The phone rang in Bud's office and Bud answered it. He put his hand over the receiver, and asks, "Do you have Bell 47 time?"

"Yes." At the same time, I was thanking God for the urge I had to stop in at Wilbur's.

It was Captain Avey Gonsolves of the **Pacific Princess** and he needed a pilot and needed one now. Avey and I spoke a few minutes on the phone getting a feel for each other. I told him I'd done most of my 2,500 hours of flying in Alaska but had also done some crop dusting with a 12-E Hiller in Oregon before that. I was forty-six now and had my own fishing business in Alaska but had never been on a tuna boat.

"How about Bell 47s? You've flown them?" Avey asked.

"Sure, no problem." I knew I was stretching the two hours I had at Wilbur's. Sometimes you can make yourself sound more confident than you are, but I hadn't lied. There had been no problems, or at least Wilbur's didn't mention any.

We met for coffee the following morning. Avey showed up in his bright red Porsche, sporting an open-neck shirt with his gold chains showing off nicely against his dark tan. Fortunately, he was many years my junior, so I grabbed at the opportunity to let him know I must have been flying when he was a little boy. He never did ask me straight out how much time I had in a Bell 47.

"We'll be leaving for Samoa in a few days," Avey said when I quizzed him. "Probably the middle of the week." I gave him Golles' number and got his.

"I'll be ready," I said as we shook hands and went our separate ways.

A JOB! I'D JUST GOTTEN A JOB! And while I hadn't a clue where Samoa was, it was finally dawning on me the immensity of what I'd just gotten myself into. My back was up against the wall. Talking was all done. The burden was now on me.

The instant Avey was out of sight, I headed for the nearest telephone. Somewhere in my travels these past weeks, an ad for learning to fly a Bell 47 (D model) had caught my attention. "$800 for ten hours of instruction."

Fortunately, I'd jotted down the number. It was in Riverside, California, nearly 200 miles away.

When the instructor answered the phone, I felt comfortable explaining the situation I was in. No matter what, I had to learn to fly that chopper this weekend.

"Come on up and we'll give her a go," he said.

I was there that evening and handed over the $800. We only had time to get some preliminaries out of the way and would start flying first thing in the morning. Two and a half hours into the instruction, he stopped me. "Look, Ted, to be honest with you, I can't teach you how to land on a tuna boat without one to practice on. You fly the helicopter fine, so I'm giving you the rest of your money back. I truly wish you the best of luck."

As I packed up my stuff and was about to head out the door, he added. "Oh yeah, let me know how it goes out there. I've always wanted to try that myself sometime."

It was a nice gesture on his part, giving me the money back like that. It certainly helped my sagging confidence, which had taken a downturn when the reality of what I'd gotten myself into actually took hold. Here I was about to go further out into the world than I'd ever been and into the Southern Hemisphere, where I'd never set foot, to be with people I knew nothing about, to fly a helicopter off a tiny moving platform on which I had no experience. I had literally put my life on the line. Not unlike free rock climbing where the climber scales cliffs with only his bare fingers. Or the NASCAR race driver going 200 mph within two inches of the wall. And what about the bull rider who climbs on the back of 2,000 pounds of fury, fully expecting to still be alive eight seconds later? I can't imagine doing any of those things and yet, inside me was that same force—the one that's inside anyone who willingly experiences life on the edge. I also fully expected I could learn to do what anyone else who flies helicopters had learned to do.

And while I may have said to Avey, "I'll be ready" like I heard the word Samoa every day, I was also thinking, *"Where the hell's Samoa?"* I left

Alaska to get a winter job flying off a tuna boat out of the harbor in sunny San Diego. I soon found out Samoa is nearly 2,000 miles more distant than Hawaii and is located in the Western Pacific. The tuna boats out of San Diego fish the Eastern Pacific. Roughly speaking, the Pacific Ocean is divided into the North Pacific, which borders the U.S., and the South Pacific bordering South America. North and South are again divided into the Eastern and Western Pacific. North being north of Hawaii and South being south of Hawaii. Papua New Guinea and Fiji are in the Western Pacific. Samoa is just a bit north and east of Fiji.

Fishing for tuna in the Eastern Pacific is entirely different than fishing for them in the West with some similarities. Yellowfin tuna like being under some kind of cover. Anything on the surface like whales, schools of dolphin or porpoise. Even boats, which is another story entirely. The technique to catch the tuna when a school of porpoise is spotted is to launch powerful high-speed, outboard-equipped skiffs from the tuna boat, which then race around and around the school to herd them into a tighter bunch. It is at that point the big seiners circle them with their net and hopefully trap the tuna under the dolphins. If there's any chop at all, it's a kidney-pounding ride for the skiff drivers who I later learned often peed blood after a session of rounding up a school of porpoise or dolphins. We'll talk about pursing the net details later, but once the net circles the rounded-up school of dolphins or porpoise, they then have to be herded back out of the net, which can be challenging as they are quite intelligent. In the process of getting them to swim or jump over and out of the net, an occasional animal might get entangled and die.

The media was quick to jump on the fact that tuna boats kill porpoise so StarKist and other companies can make money. The evening news zeroed in on such events when they happened. "**Dolphin Free**" became a big selling point for tuna everywhere.

It was the Japanese with their sophisticated electronic equipment who figured out a solution. The floating logs in the Western Pacific also held tuna.

No worry about killing dolphins and porpoise with log fishing. And so, the Western Pacific fishery was born. The **Pacific Princess** had only made the switch a few years before I arrived on the scene. The switch was so sudden, some of the Peruvian crew members never even knew it was happening. All of a sudden, they found themselves in Samoa.

The logs were actually saw logs that somehow were lost in logging operations around the world. I knew Alaska and British Columbia were famous for bunching logs together into huge rafts after they slid down the mountain and into the ocean. At that point they were towed to mills. Storms happen and logs get loose. Did the logs in the Western Pacific come all the way from Alaska? Or were they from logging operations in New Guinea, New Zealand, or maybe Northern Australia? I never learned. But they were certainly there. And the one thing I soon learned about the logs we encountered is that sharks also liked to congregate under logs. So, if ever you are shipwrecked or downed in an airplane, and survive and manage to find a log to crawl up on to save your life, it better be a big one because just below the surface, there will be sharks!

CHAPTER 2

PAGO PAGO
(PRONOUNCED PANGO PANGO)

Wednesday, January 30, 1985
(Somewhere out over the Pacific)

Finally, I'm on a jet heading to American Samoa. My goals: fly safe, fly lots, and write down my feelings as much as possible. But the stark reality of what I'd just gotten myself into was strong. Here I was on my way further than I'd ever ventured out into the world, where I'd never set foot, to be with people I didn't know, to fly a helicopter with only minimal experience in more years than I could remember. I figured the part about landing on a moving boat at sea was a bridge I'd have to cross when the time came.

It's a long way from San Diego to Samoa. You fly to Hawaii from the West Coast and then fly that far again in the same general direction before you finally arrive at Pago Pago. Samoa has one of the finest deep-water protected harbors in the entire Western Pacific and is strategically located for shipping canned tuna back to the U.S. It was the perfect place for StarKist to build another processing plant.

There were at least a dozen or more super seiners tied up in the harbor when I arrived. Most were not fishing. Something about a cutback in the price of tuna and there not being the markets of a few years prior. It seemed everyone had a net mending needle in their hand or sticking out of their pocket as the huge seines were off-loaded or put aboard. When I inquired about their size, I began to realize that I had gotten myself involved in something that was hard to fathom. Nearly a mile long and weighing a hundred tons, they were each worth a million dollars. Add the cost of the net to a boat valued in the ten-million-dollar range and all of a sudden, my little thirty-two-foot operation in Alaska seemed insignificant. On a world scale, fishing was an unbelievably huge business. But it was the afternoon tropical showers and evening breezes I enjoyed most about being there.

Samoans, Peruvians, and Portuguese were involved in most of the activities and I heard we would be competing with the Japanese and Poles as well. Our Portuguese navigator had fished tuna off the coast of Africa, and we had Chiu, a master Chinese chef. I was truly at some sort of an international crossroads out here on this tiny island so far from anything I knew. Despite the language barriers and the catchy melodic music playing on all the open window busses, the different races had one thing in common—everything was measured in American dollars. It hadn't always been that way. Fine mats used to be the symbol of wealth here before it became an American colony and big business pushed its way in. The tuna boats were here because StarKist had built their cannery in this beautiful natural harbor, where the palm trees swayed and the beaches showed the first signs of pollution with the litter that washed up each morning. They had moved their San Diego operation here to avoid the high American labor costs and were now no doubt taking advantage of a people who annually could live on three thousand dollars.

The only reason the **Pacific Princess** was fishing was that StarKist owned half the boat. Avey Gonsolves' father owned the other half. Avey was the fish captain on board and had no doubt been declared the captain by his dad. You don't need any license to call the shots on a boat but you do need lots of paperwork and years of experience to get a 1,100 ton or more Master's License, and his dad's brother (better known as Father John) was the Master of the boat. He probably had enough paperwork to captain the **Queen Mary**. It was Father John who took your passport away from you the instant you stepped on board. From that point on, your only country was the deck boards under your feet.

Thursday, January 31, 1985
(Pago Pago)

First day on board and much to learn. I was shown my quarters, which I'd be sharing with two others—the helicopter mechanic Ray Johnson and the navigator Raymond Falante. Normally the assistant to the chief engineer would also have been there but Ray Johnson was doing double duty on this trip and would be the engineer's assistant as well as take care of any maintenance on the helicopter. There were two sets of bunk beds in the room. We had our own bathroom with a very nice shower and our own TV where we could watch videos from time to time. I never saw any other quarters, except engineer Andy White's. I knew Avey had his own apartment just under the flying bridge and Father John had a private room somewhere on the boat though I never learned where. Right across the hall from our room was Andy's and it too was private. All the crew members shared rooms as well as bathrooms. Andy was alone because the engine room always had someone on watch in case something went awry. The watchman would set off an alarm, which rang a loud bell right by Andy's bed and he would be there in seconds. I think he slept in his clothes. The night he was called to put out an engine room fire, I never heard a thing from right across the hallway. Andy had the situation under control before anyone else could react. Andy, I was to learn, was a mechanical genius but we'll get into that a bit later. Andy did take me down to his workshop at some point to show me all the tools, saying I could use the shop whenever I wanted. There was an old sperm whale's tooth lying on a bench that was broken. "If you want that, you can have it." I'd always wanted to try carving some ivory. Scrimshaw work seemed way out of my reach, but who knows?

I was finally taken out to see the chopper at the airport and meet the two Kiwis (Chris and Brit) who had been flown in from New Zealand to get it flyable. They were the first Kiwis I'd ever met. Lots of characters in a place like this.

My first look at the helicopter took my breath away. It had encountered a rotor strike on the last trip. Fortunately, it wasn't flying at the time. They had run into some nasty weather on the way home and the rotor blade tie-downs had snapped loose in the middle of the night, which let the blades start turning faster and faster in the high winds. Evidently the boat came crashing down from a big wave and the rotor blade struck the tail boom which would be an invitation to die if it happened in the air. With the floats sagging the way they were, disaster isn't a strong enough word for what was before me. I hoped the parts got here soon!

Chiu (the Chinese chef) and I took the bus to town to find some tennis shoes for me (all of seven dollars while probably thirty-seven in Anchorage) and some ginseng for Father John. I later took the bus again out into the countryside where it made a loop back into town. The melodic music and the open windows were delightful. I noticed a Samoan woman sitting in the shade of a palm tree as we passed. She was quietly gazing out at apparently nothing. Forty-five minutes later when the bus returned, she was still in exactly the same position. I saw others along the way sitting and weaving mats. Fine mats were once, as I already mentioned, the currency of Samoa. A person's wealth was judged by how tall was the stack of mats they owned. One thing that really got my attention was that none of the houses had walls. I later learned the houses are called fales. All have thatched roofs. Everything was open to the weather. Not very private I thought but I also noticed the rolled-up mats hanging up next to the would-be ceiling that could be rolled down if need be. Coming from Alaska's cold, seeing no walls in a house was definitely a first. I was so fixed on cold, I couldn't bring myself to leave my wool shirt behind with the other stuff I'd left in San Diego. Trust me. You don't need a wool shirt in Samoa! It is definitely a tropical South Sea island with rain showers off and on all day plus it's very hot and muggy. Even burned my bald top today. Hope to get downtown at some point to see the museum. As much of a tropical paradise as this seems, I'm sure without speaking the native tongue and getting to know the locals, living here would be a drag. Although hunting fruit bats is available as well as snorkeling and diving, so maybe a guy could entertain himself for some time.

The Samoan people are very laid-back. Sort of refreshing. It is very common to see people just sitting or lounging around mid-day, afternoon, anytime. Of course, there isn't a lot to do here as we Westerners (maybe we're actually Easterners now that I think of it) are programmed to believe we must be doing something every second. They worry about eating and sleeping and keeping the rain off their heads. That's it! I did see some gardens and nice yards from my bus ride, so that may not be entirely accurate.

The bus was very pleasant. Polynesian music via the driver's boom box seemed to promote a very polite atmosphere. All women get a seat. If there's a question, the men automatically get up and move to the rear or stand in the doorway. It was nice to see it happening. Older women get the front seats.

The guys, helicopter mechanic Ray Johnson, engineer Andy White, and Raymond Falante, the navigator, and I all went out for hamburgers and a beer that night at a thatched roof bar with no walls. It was fun talking with them one on one without all the hubbub on the *Princess* and having the South Sea's warm evening breezes brushing my skin. I enjoyed the evening very much.

Friday, February 1, 1985
(Pago Pago)

I got in an early morning swim with a few of the locals at a nearby beach that had a fresh water shower before heading out to the helicopter. I'd never swam in eighty-five-degree water before and it was nice to shower afterwards. I'd also never seen anyone who had what looked like their clothes tattooed onto their bodies. The two men I saw showering were solidly tattooed from the waist to their feet. I later learned from one of the Samoans on the boat that you can never go through that alone but always have to have a partner or you would die from the pain.

Spent the rest of the day putzing on the helicopter. It was amazing how much the Kiwis had accomplished since I'd left them yesterday.

Saturday, February 2, 1985
(Still helicoptering)

Tracking the rotor blades is something I'd always known about but had never witnessed. It's what makes for a very smooth operating machine. Simply put, one of the mechanics is perched at the top of a stepladder just inches from the spinning rotor blades with a pencil in his hand, and carefully puts a mark on the tip of the blades as they whir past him at 400 rpms. The helicopter is stopped and the blades are walked around by the second person past a fixed point on the step ladder. Each pencil mark has to pass exactly through the fixed mark on the ladder. If that's not the case, an adjustment is made, the helicopter is started up again, and the whole process is repeated until they get it perfect. My job in all this was operating the chopper. When I finally got to take it for a test flight, it was the smoothest flying helicopter I'd ever been in. As I implied earlier, those Kiwis knew what they were doing. By late afternoon and several more practice sessions, word came down that it was time to put the bird on the boat. The helicopter flew very well, except for the sticky throttle, which was to be fixed soon. The Kiwis and I exchanged addresses and bid our G'days. Who knows if we'll ever cross paths again?

At five-thirty p.m. the chopper was securely chained down to the topmost deck sticky throttle and all (tach time was 2274.7). Avey had promised me some practice time before we left the harbor. I'd learned long before not to depend on anyone's promises and was not in the least bit bashful about asking for advice from any pilot I met around the harbor about landing on a boat at sea. I was glad I did.

Pilots are members of a fraternity of sorts—especially if you're not afraid to admit you're scared. Everyone who flies has known fear at one time or another. How we all handle that fear is another matter. No pilot ever failed to open up to me in response to something I was unsure about. Landing on a tuna boat at sea was unknown to me. The pitching of the boat as it plowed along through the waves at the standard thirteen knots, sometimes moving up and down as much as ten feet or more while rolling from side to side, was not to be underestimated in the least. "Be careful" was the common denominator in every conversation I had on that subject.

Saturday evening, we all, the two Rays, Andy, me, Father John, and Avey, went out to a Polynesian floor show and dinner. Father John was known wherever we went and evidently well liked. He had thirty-five years at sea, a wife, and seven kids at home. Avey picked up the tab. Nice!

CHAPTER 3

FIRST FLIGHT

Sunday, February 3, 1985
(Goodbye to Pago Pago)

It was one-thirty p.m. when the **Pacific Princess**, its side thrusters churning, eased away from the dock in Pago Pago and sailed out of the harbor. Avey had forgotten about the practice session he had promised in his rush to get underway. Here I was with only a single landing to my credit while the boat was still firmly tied to the dock, and now here we were, headed out into the wide-open Pacific for real. Regardless, going out to sea was definitely a big event for me. I sat up in the chopper pretending I was on a Polynesian cruise—which I was. It was beautiful sailing past the other islands of Western Samoa with the way the afternoon sun was striking the vividly blue water. The boat then pointed its bow to the northwest and parts unknown.

Boats are much different than ships. I don't know for sure where the definition of one ends and the other begins, but I would suspect it's in the brain. Certainly, someone who sailed many years on this 250,000-ton monster and then came aboard my thirty-two-foot gill netter in Alaska would know he was on a boat. The same would be true, I'm sure, of an old Navy captain after spending years aboard a destroyer and then shipping out on the **Pacific Princess**.

To me, I was on board the most beautiful ship in the world and taking the South Pacific cruise of a lifetime. The tropics. I had been to Hawaii once but that was as far south as I'd ever been. The Southern Cross would have to be pointed out to me here. The North Star which I'd looked up to my whole life now guided the other half of the world. Here, below the equator, if water really did swirl down the drain in the opposite direction, what would it do right on the line? If I got a chance, I would find out.

We had another imaginary line out in front of us as well. Off to the west was the International Date Line where you could sail into tomorrow and back into yesterday if you wanted. And while I'd studied navigation in two fields, there was going to be no shortage of things to learn here. Provided of course, I could learn to land the chopper back on its high perch while we continued to gently roll our way through these shark-infested beautiful blue waters where the horizon never changed. It was always there stretching endlessly over the curve that sailors once knew to be the edge of the earth.

We'd be passing through the Solomon Islands where JFK's time aboard a torpedo boat took place. New Guinea was out there as well. I'd read countless stories about the head hunters who still plied its unmapped jungles. And north was Guam. Vast expanses of ocean lay between all these and this is where we planned to fill the boat with tuna.

The Western Pacific tuna fishery started happening in the 1980s when the Japanese, with their super sophisticated electronics, learned that floating logs often held schools of tuna just as had the pods of dolphins and shoals of porpoise in the Eastern Pacific. The bigger and older the log, the better. Even whales held tuna under them. Tuna evidently like to cluster under anything—even boats. The bad publicity of occasionally killing a dolphin or porpoise in the process of netting a school of StarKist tuna finally wasn't worth it, which is how Pago Pago came into the picture.

The Eastern Pacific extended from the western side of the U.S. to off the coast of Peru and beyond, so tuna definitely was widespread.

As mentioned earlier, our navigator Raymond Falante had once fished for tuna off the coast of Africa with his dad. Unfortunately, the Peruvians on board the *Princess* weren't even notified the boat was transferring to the

Western Pacific when the move happened. At least one on board, when I was there, hadn't seen his family in two years.

We sailed on into the night a second time. By then we were well clear of any landfall that could be reached with the chopper. Once off the deck, I would have one hour forty-five minutes to figure how to get it safely back on board, before getting into the fifteen minutes of reserve fuel that everyone had cautioned me to guard with my life. At most, I would have two hours before the engine quit.

On the third day, Avey's voice came over the intercom. "Warm it up, Ted." He'd finally remembered our practice session. The procedure was simple enough. First the call would come over the speakers throughout the ship. I'd drop whatever I was doing and head to the top deck to be met by Filipo, the Samoan boy who would be responsible for hooking and unhooking the tie-down chains whenever we arrived or departed. Together we would do any last-minute items like untying the main rotor blades and the tail rotor. I'd check the oil and fuel once more and then climb aboard, while getting into my Mae West (life jacket), and then buckle myself in.

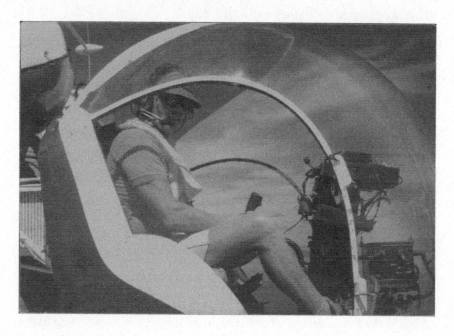

Filipo would then remove the doors and store them safely below deck, before giving me the thumbs-up sign that it was all clear to start the engine to warm it up. Avey would show up a few minutes later and buckle himself in but he would never put on his Mae West.

"*He was the captain and could do as he pleased,*" I thought. But if this bucket of bolts hit the water, even though we carried a life raft, flares, a special homing beeper, and other electronic gear, if we were unconscious in the water, none of it would be worth a darn. At least I wanted to be floating.

In Alaska, just going into the water meant almost certain death from exposure unless you got into your survival suit. Here, we flew in shorts and sandals—the 85-degree water so inviting you almost wanted to be in it. This was different all right but surviving a ditching at sea in an aircraft was not something to be taken lightly—especially one with rotating blades that could cut you to pieces. And even though the helicopter was equipped with pontoons, my experience landing on water with them was nil. To date, I had zero experience either flying off or landing on a boat at sea. Period!

When the engine temperature hit the green and I'd checked the mags, I nodded to Filipo and he unfastened the back chain on my side and walked around the front of the bubble and did the same on Avey's side. We were half ready to go. The sweat streaming down my sides and soaking my flying gloves was not from tropical heat. We still had two more chains to unfasten.

Meanwhile, I checked in with Father John down in the wheelhouse via the radio. He was the master on board and carried all the legal papers to operate in international waters and would be our only link back to the boat once we left. As we made the radio checks, he gave me the wind direction and speed. He then asked which way I wanted him to steer the ship to best take advantage of the thirteen knots the **Princess** was making as it plowed through the gentle swells in the tropical sun-filled morning. There was nothing on the horizon except the gentle curve of the earth.

The old Bell 47 had all it could do to develop enough horsepower with its reciprocating engine—even at red line—to get off the deck if it was especially hot and muggy and there was no wind. And even though some turbulence was created as our own thirteen-knot wind slammed into the ship's structure, it was safer to have this added breeze than not on most days.

So, when the engine was warmed up and the radio checks were completed, I shifted my gaze to the wind sock out on the bow and watched the oncoming swells roll under us. The swells are always there no matter how flat the sea looks. Father John watched the wind sock as well and kept the bow of the *Princess* pointed accordingly. Nervously I watched and waited for things to smooth out a bit and then nodded to Filipo, who was squatting in front of the bubble, plugging his ears with his fingers against the engine noise. He quickly jumped up and removed the last chain from my side and then Avey's, at which point he gave us the "all clear" sign and left the deck. I visually checked to see that my side was clear of chains by leaning out the door and looking and gave Avey the thumbs-up. He then did the same for me. Leaving a chain attached when in a hurry to leave the deck was an invitation to die. There is a thing in helicopter circles known as a dynamic roll-over. It is technically difficult to explain and once initiated, even more difficult to correct with very few pilots being quick enough to react. Simply put, it meant autorotating back to the deck which you never left in the first place. As I said, it was complicated and was much easier to avoid in the first place by double-checking the chains.

When I got Avey's thumbs-up signal, I pulled the collective and gently pushed forward on the cyclic. We rose off the deck and over the port side in one swooping motion. The old Bell helicopter had done that many times over the years, and as we moved away on the invisible bubble of air and I looked around, the giant 220-foot, 1,100-ton-capacity super seiner that had appeared so massive at the dock was transformed into a boat and a tiny one at that.

Like it or not, my first lesson in landing on a moving platform at sea was underway. I had talked with everyone I could find who knew anything at all about what I could expect to happen once I left the ship but nothing had come close to preparing me for this moment. I had put my life on the line once again and could feel its vibrance pulsing within me. Even my soul was committed.

Completing a wide circle out and away from the **Princess**, I could sense every one of the remaining souls on board were glued to every porthole and rail on the starboard side to watch the newcomer from Alaska attempt his first landing.

Once more the massive bulk of the ship was there as we eased up close, hovering just out of reach of its steel and aluminum sides. Here it wasn't submissively tied to its berth at the dock. Free and at sea, it was a vibrant creature. From the vantage point of a helicopter hanging magically in thin air, inches from its grasp, the sight was menacing. By hovering level along its edge, it was easy to measure the height of the swell as the top deck rose above our pontoons only to pitch back down as the ship's hull plunged once more into the mile-deep, blue water below us. Father John drove the *Princess* into the breeze that came up from the south. The wind sock was holding true for a diagonal landing across the deck that was required to miss the twenty-six antennas that sprouted from all points aft. I knew how many there were because I had deliberately counted them during my long worried wait for this moment.

Tuna boats are all equipped with a high mast and a powerful hydraulic block designed in such a way as to grab hold of the cork line and winch the net back aboard. The boom is movable so the operator can keep repositioning the net as it hangs down from the block to aid the crew stacking the net below. It is an exacting job because the net once stacked has to be ready to be laid out again. The crow's nest sits atop a hollow tower very close to the main boom with a ladder inside so anyone can climb up into it through the trap door in its floor. The crow's nest tower also has a couple of lesser booms attached to it near the bottom and equipped with winches used to lower the high-powered skiffs into the water or the huge dip net used to bring the trapped tuna out of the pursed net and onto the deck. Two observers with their big binoculars are stationed in the crow's nest every daylight hour of every day if the boat is moving. I knew those two guys had the best seats in town for the show at hand, but as long as I could keep the chopper out in front of them and down on the deck, all would be OK. The problem was how to get over the edge of the pitching, rolling platform without catching a pontoon, while hovering at the same speed as the *Princess*. The trick, I had been told, was to aim for and hit the small, red-circled "T" that was painted on the center of the platform. Everything else was supposed to fall into place after that.

Your entire concentration had to be focused on that small "T." Almost. There was still the helicopter to fly: RPMs to monitor, manifold pressure to check, the turbulence of the air coming across the deck, and the deck itself that never stopped coming up to grab a chunk of us as we hung there waiting and calculating for the right moment. A technique had been developed that helped overcome all this, but it took experience which I didn't have.

Still, we all have to start from somewhere and I'd already been airborne for nearly fifteen minutes as the clock methodically ticked away at our precious fuel supply.

The technique, as it was explained to me, was to focus your eyes totally on the tiny red circle making it your whole immediate world. Everything else you had to sense rather than see. By focusing on the circle, your brain automatically would transform it into an immovable landing zone, much as the runway would be on land, where your eyes then are actually focused on the horizon. If you looked at the horizon here, even for a second, the boat would drive out from under you, bringing along all its antennas, mast, and booms, which could more than ruin your day.

The time had come. I positioned the helicopter a few feet above the highest point to which the deck was pushed skyward by the swells, and hovered diagonally along, keeping pace with the boat but now my attention was focused totally on the spot. When the *Princess* reached its apex on what I calculated to be one of the smaller swells, I headed for the little red "T" in the center of the circle and never took my eyes away, almost feeling my way there.

The idea was to be solidly down on the deck before it started its next upward thrust. Ideally, meeting it on the way down gave you the softest landing. If for some reason you hurried the procedure, you would likely overshoot the spot. The rule then was to go around. It is the most prudent rule in aviation.

On my fifth go around, Avey said, "Want me to show you how I do it?"

"Yes, by all means!"

Now I knew Avey did not have a license to fly, but dual controls were common in all the choppers I'd seen. It is always nice to be able to give someone else the controls so you can take a break now and then.

I was only too glad to be able to pry my fingers loose and let some warmth come back into them once again. My armpits might have been dripping but in my fingers was the cold reality of what was happening around me.

Avey had tons of hours of chopper time from a string of pilots over the years who had been willing to give him lessons. He made it look deceptively easy. I'd been hurrying over that terrifying edge much too quickly to be under control in time to hit the spot. "Av" gently set her down right on the "T."

"*So that's how it's done*," I thought to myself and off the deck we went again. This time I swallowed hard and dragged us over the edge. The landing was a little rough but I hit dead center in the middle of the ocean on top of that tiny red circle. My first successful landing at sea was now history. But it would never get easy. Later, I would hear myself giving the same warnings that I had gotten when anyone approached me about flying off a tuna boat. "Be careful!" was about all I could tell them.

CHAPTER 4

WESTERN PACIFIC FISHING GROUNDS

Tuesday, February 5, 1985
(Still near Western Samoa)

Up at four a.m. Close to the log now. Boat only jogging. Then the command, "*Let it go.*" Finally, our first set! Real excitement now. A BIG, BIG operation! A mile of net going out, weighing 100 tons, peeling off the back of the *Princess* like it was nothing. Of course, the *Princess* was "black smoking it," meaning it was under full power with the thirty-two-foot sein skiff doing the same in the opposite direction. Net and cables flying everywhere.

That's the thumbnail version. Evidently, the boat had been tracking a beeper-marked log from the time we left Pago Pago and had found it sometime during the night. The four a.m. alarm was a surprise to me but not to the crew. This is what they did for a living. I soon found myself up in the "crow's nest" where Avey had long before positioned himself. Nothing was random. The net was let go at exactly twenty minutes before sunrise so that it was pursed up before there was too much daylight. Any later and the tuna they were trying to catch would have easily seen what was going on and escaped out the bottom of the net. The entire operation, known as a "set," was a choreographed dance of sorts. While Father John was jogging the *Princess* to get into position, Macho and Mace had climbed into the sein skiff that was precariously perched on its special platform up against the huge pile of stacked net on the stern of the **Princess.** The big skiff was towed into place by a powerful winch and cable and securely locked into place with a special mechanism that needed to be slammed with a heavy sledge hammer to release it. Mace was at the ready with the sledge while Macho had the engine running in the skiff waiting for the command from Avey to "LET IT GO." At that instant, there was a very loud boom as Mace hit the release mechanism with the sledge and the skiff started its backward slide down into the water dragging the net tow lines with it. That's when Father John hit the throttle to full power and the net started peeling off the back of the **Princess.** Macho immediately turned the skiff around and also hit full power. While it looked like the skiff was pulling the net off the **Princess**, it was actually the twelve-cylinder locomotive engine powering the **Princess** through its twelve inch diameter shaft and huge propeller that did the work.

The seine skiff added drag as Macho almost immediately started turning the skiff to the right which started the circle but Father John dutifully took his commands from Avey in the crow's nest. Calling down to his uncle, Avey said, "OK, start turning, Unk." Father John would then slowly turn to port to start completing the mile long circle of net streaming off the back of the boat. Everyone on board couldn't help but hear Noli's shouted warning over the intercom, "HALF NET" as the half way mark sped by. Noli (in the dark t-shirt) was the deck boss which meant just that.

When Macho and Father John met up, Mace, the guy who slammed the sledge hammer that started this whole thing, would hand the skiff's tow lines to someone on board the *Princess* and immediately Macho would drive the skiff to the starboard side where another deckhand passed them two more tow lines. This time, one line was connected to the bow and another to the stern of the *Princess.* Macho and Mace's job then was to tug on the lines in whichever direction the *Princess* needed to move to keep it from being pulled into the net. The net was now busily being pursed and brought aboard with many hands pulling and stacking in a prescribed pile. Everyone not stacking the net knew their job.

Meanwhile, another skiff (a high-speed outboard) was lowered into the water from the starboard side with a couple of hands aboard. Their job was to drag the circled log out of the ever-tightening circle of net.

When they finally got the log close to the cork line near the boat, other crewmembers on the *Princess* started jumping into the water to hold the net down as the skiff towed the log away. If you saw the guys scrambling up onto the cork line, or trying frantically to climb into the skiff, you can be sure one of them spied a whitetip shark. The story of a crewmember from another boat years before, all too vivid in their memory. The whitetip grabbed the kid, who happened to be the captain's son, by the shoulder and while they managed to get him out of the water, he didn't survive. Whitetips were feared by all.

When the log was clear of the net and pursing nearly complete, Macho and Mace handed their lines back to someone on the *Princess*. They then came back around to the port side and up close to the net, where a huge long-handled dip net was lowered to them from another of the lesser booms and winches manned by Noli.

Macho and Mace's job now was to plunge the dip net down into the fish that were now visible inside the net. Their muscles glistened in the morning sun as they pushed the net with everything they had down into the ball of fish. On their signal to Noli, the net, which could hold a ton or more of tuna, was raised up and lifted just above a fish container (which looked like an open topped box) on the deck where it was dumped so other crewmembers could take out the untargeted fish species.

They only wanted the tuna. Andy, the engineer, was busy taking temperature samples of one here and there before they plunged down a trough to the freezing water waiting below in the fish hold. Andy was the one who made the decision whether a fish was kept or not. Evidently, the temperature of the fish coming directly out of the school just captured was very critical on whether it could be flash frozen safely.

From the point the tuna were dumped on board, it was Andy's job to care for them until they were unloaded back in Pago Pago. He'd prepared the below-freezing water by adding salt. Lots of it. Once the tuna were frozen solid, the now slimy water would be pumped to the next fish hold and the fish just flash frozen would remain frozen just as they would in any freezer. Andy would again make the calculations to the slimy water to ensure enough additional salt was added to keep the liquid at below freezing. Suffice it to say, caring for a million-dollar load of StarKist's tuna plus the entire operation of the 10-million-dollar boat that caught and held them was a huge responsibility. Andy's paycheck was something like $30,000 or more for every trip he took and he was worth every penny. We netted thirty-five tons on this first set. It was a start.

Mechanical genius probably isn't enough of an accolade for chief engineer Andy White. He was always busy fixing something.

Tuna boats all have five compressors on board to ensure that in case of a breakdown of one, there's another working one to take its place. The importance of the compressors cannot be emphasized enough. The fish needed to be kept frozen at all costs. Andy told me some boats limp into Pago Pago with all five compressors operating at full capacity while Andy never had to use more than two to keep the load frozen and the crew comfortable. Other boats were putting a lot on the line with all five compressors at full capacity. Evidently, the chlorine in the refrigerant would pit the tiny valves in the compressors that regulated the compressor's efficiency and Andy was quick to figure that out. By cleaning the pitting in the valves using the shop's metal lathe (Andy used his index finger and thumb held a little over an inch apart to give me some reference to how big they were), he was able to keep his compressors operating at peak performance at all times. Best part was he always had three compressors standing by for any emergency that might happen at sea. Not many boats were able to say that.

The time from "let it go" to the last bit of net and fish aboard and the clean-up involved could be anywhere from two to more hours. Everything depended on the number of fish in the net or any problems they might encounter. Some days the net was set out six or more times! The crew also earned every penny.

Time for breakfast.

CHAPTER 5

CHIU (SAME GENERAL AREA)

The ship's galley on the **Princess** I soon learned was the hub of the boat. Oh yes, the wheelhouse where Father John and the navigator Falante hung out with all the high-tech radio/navigation equipment was control central for the boat, but the real energy on board happened in the galley. The entire crew could be assembled there at any time for pep talks, for a movie, or while the authorities in Samoa searched the boat for drugs, which actually happened but that's another story entirely. Thanks to the boat's chef Chiu, the meals were always first rate. He was always cleaning fish or cooking outside on the deck if at all possible.

Chiu also brought another nationality on board. His parents had carried him on their backs when they were escaping Mainland China at the end of the Second World War. Chiu's dad had worked for Chiang Kai-shek and had to leave the country or risk being killed. Their goal was to get to Formosa, known today as Taiwan, where American ships were waiting to take them and thousands of others fleeing the country. Food was scarce as they made their way across the country to the waiting boats. If they got desperate, they would buy a kilo-size can of meat, which cost an ounce of gold. Chinese know a lot about gold. The ships waiting for them knew about gold, too. The cost to get a ticket out to safety was another ounce of gold for each person, regardless of their age. These courageous people who had assisted the Americans in their war effort had now been reduced to dollar signs. And it didn't end when they boarded the ships. There was very little in the way of aid when they finally landed on the island. Food was still scarce. So scarce, they had to start their own gardens in order to eat. Chiu's dad insisted he attend school no matter what and some days a single turnip was all he got to eat. He said his head was sometimes spinning because he was so hungry, but he stayed in school.

Later in life, Chiu found himself still struggling and while I didn't get all the details, he must have become a chef along the way and eventually found someone who could get him a chef's job in the U.S. He signed a contract and soon found himself working in California. What Chiu hadn't realized at the time was the contract was for life. He was "owned" by what amounts to the Chinese mafia, although he didn't use those words, but his escape from all that is how he came to be on board the *Pacific Princess*.

Chiu had a Samoan helper named Masalino, known in other circles as the bull cook, although I never actually saw him do any actual cooking.

Masalino is on the left. That's Mace beside him. Masalino also helped stack net on the back deck and when he wasn't doing that, he was peeling garlic, or washing pots and pans, or stacking the dish washer, or emptying trash. I couldn't help but marvel at the quantity of garlic on board. An apple box filled to the top is a huge pile of garlic, some of which was not for food. Always some was superstitiously hung on the railings near the bow to ward off evil spirits or danger or whatever (I never actually heard for sure). Before our trip was over, we got resupplied with more garlic from another boat going home. Several other boats going home supplied us with additional fuel, which we'll talk about later.

Breakfast was usually at seven a.m., but if we circled a log that morning, it was a hit and miss operation. Guys came and went as they could. The Samoans almost always chose Top Ramen noodles, even though bacon and eggs and toast were always available. Sometimes it was pancakes and there was even a waffle maker. Lunches almost always included sashimi, which, on the *Pacific Princess*, was raw, cut-up tuna. While Chiu served a wide variety of entrees in the evening, his BBQ tuna bellies will always be one of the top three meals of my entire life. And while I watched Masalino peel garlic with his thumb nail and index finger every day, Chiu incorporated it in such a way you never felt overpowered by its taste. His food was delicious!

Breakfast could be anything from soup to eggs, raw fish to cold cereal, sweet rolls or fresh bread, and orange juice. Usually, all of the above, including fried fish.

Lunch today was hamburgers, clam chowder, fish (raw), tuna salad, salad (with lettuce, onions, tomatoes, carrots, celery, and peppers), fresh rolls, leftover fried fish, french fries, cupcakes, and watermelon. Kool-Aid to drink is the usual—also milk.

Dinner last night was shish kabobs. Always salad, always rice, and usually potatoes and most of the stuff from lunch, too. Later in the evening, particularly during movies, there was always ice cream. How much ice cream we went through on our trip would have been an interesting fact to know. I do know I was not drinking coffee, when I came on board, but a bowl of vanilla ice cream before going to bed with a cup of coffee nearby so you could dunk a spoonful of ice cream in it had me hooked in no time.

CHAPTER 6

THE SEARCH BEGINS

Wednesday, February 6, 1985
(Still near our 1st set)

At sea now four days. Still messing with some logs near our 1st set. Another ten tons today. One hatch is full, so there will be a hatch party tonight. So far boat life isn't too bad. Getting used to the movement of the boat. Sort of strange up on the deck at night with the stars constantly swaying back and forth like they do. Really liking the warm evening breezes and hearing the gentle crunching of the chopper as it moves the inflatable floats with the swaying. Very relaxing for me.

Thursday, February 7, 1985
(3:30 p.m.)

Flew one hour this morning. The flying is feeling better all the time. I take photos of Filipo and Kiso. Their heads got shaved last night. A ritual of the first trip. Hope I'm not next. Gulp!

Friday, February 8, 1985
(Slightly west of yesterday)

We are now officially searching for logs that could be holding tuna but also for breezers and foamers as well as whales. The breezers and foamers had to be explained to me. These are the free schools of tuna not associated with logs. Bird activity can give them away so we were always looking for birds as well. If you look out over smooth water and see what appears to be ripples like what would happen if a slight breeze was disturbing the surface—especially if you see birds, you certainly needed to go check it out. I'm not quite sure what the fish are thinking but they come to the surface and thrash around a bit, then dive back down into the depths for several minutes and then resurface and do it over again. These schools are catchable if you time the dives and the surfacing so you can get your net around them at the right time. Foamers are fish actively feeding on the surface. If the wind is just right, the odor of fish in the air can be very strong. Avey and I once got to see a sperm whale come up through a foamer with its mouth wide open so full of tuna that they were spilling out both sides. What a bad time to not have your camera!

Now for the search itself. No matter where the *Princess* was going, two observers were always up in the bird's nest every daylight hour with powerful field glasses (literally eighteen to twenty inches long and heavy). These glasses could easily let the user see out ten miles or more. Avey carried a pair in the chopper as well. There were even larger, more powerful binoculars mounted to the gunwales on either side of the boat. The searching was not a haphazard event. It was more like a choreographed dance. Before leaving the top deck of the boat, Father John and I would do our radio check for the search. Every five minutes from that point on, he would call me with two numbers—miles out and magnetic heading back to the boat. I would answer him repeating the two numbers at the same time jotting them down on my kneepad. My reply was brief. For example: "Roger, twenty out, one eighty-seven return." If for any reason one of us didn't reply within the five minutes, the other was to immediately head to where the last transmission stated. Either the radios were down or we were in the water. At twenty miles out, it would take the *Princess* over an hour and half to get to us but only fifteen minutes for us to get back to them.

There was a transponder on board the *Princess* that identified us over any other choppers that may be in the area and while we rarely saw another boat, I knew they were around because we were part of a radio group of maybe a dozen boats that talked in code to each other every evening. Everyone in that group knew the whereabouts of every other boat and knew what they were seeing and how many fish, if any, they netted that day.

Since the guys in the tower could easily cover the ten miles on either side of the boat, Avey and I would fly out twenty miles to the starboard and then make a left turn paralleling the direction of the *Princess*. It was set up this way because helicopters are flown from the right seat. As I mentioned, Avey also had a pair of the heavy binocs, so he could cover the additional ten miles we were out from the bird's nest observers. We had an hour and forty-five minutes of fuel to spend in the search plus the fifteen minutes in reserve, which I'd been cautioned many times to *guard* with my life. Every five minutes I'd get the call from Father John, I'd roger him while jotting the numbers on my kneepad and on we'd go. Since we were travelling nearly five times faster than the *Princess*, a system had been perfected to let us fly a circle (in the form of a box) around the boat and be back before our one hour and forty-five minutes of fuel was used up. At that point, we were again at the side of the 250,000-ton monster where another treacherous spot landing awaited. Filipo was always there to immediately chain the chopper to the deck and would then busy himself replacing the doors, topping the tanks off with fuel or whatever else needed doing. If it was time for lunch, we got to take a break and maybe even a nap for Ted. And then sometime later, I'd hear, "Warm it up, Ted," and the whole process would repeat itself in the afternoon. This might go on for days but if we happened to spot a log, lots of things changed. Avey would inform his uncle that we were going down to check out a log. The first thing Avey would have me do when we descended from our 1,000-foot perch was to hover very close to the log where the wind from the rotor blades would thrash the surface of the water. Baitfish also sought refuge under and around logs as well as did sharks. The turbulent water would have the baitfish coming up from the depths in droves to see what was going on. If the baitfish were there, chances were tuna would be there as well. But we needed the *Princess* with its underwater side-scanning sonar to come and find the log to check it out. To assist in that, we carried a special homing beeper strapped under the helicopter. The first thing Avey would do is reach out on the side racks and retrieve his speargun, which was tethered to the beeper with a cord. He'd harpoon the log with the speargun and pull another cord with a specially tied knot that loosed the beeper into the water and then call his uncle to let him know the beeper was deployed. Father John would then call the beeper on a frequency that made an actual beep in a prearranged sequence. Father John's signal might be two short beeps and three long ones. Immediately the beeper we'd just deployed would answer with the identical sequence and then go silent. When Father John heard the signal, he'd turn the **Princess** in the direction of the beeper and Avey and I would head back to the boat, intercepting it somewhere along the way and making our landing. When the **Princess** arrived at the scene, someone in the wheelhouse would lower the side-scanning radar and Father John would position the **Princess** out several hundred yards and slowly drive around the log. If it showed promise, another whole sequence of events was put into action.

We carried an array of bamboo logs on deck plus what they called a floating light raft equipped with a generator that powered an array of bright lights hung around the raft and aimed where they would shine down into the water. It was a ploy to trick the baitfish into thinking something was going on, hoping the tuna would stay there as well. The raft was lowered from the deck and into the water as was an outboard skiff with a couple of guys on board. Their job was to tow the raft to the log where it was secured with a stout line. If it was late enough in the day, the generator would be fired up with its lights aglow. If not, the skiff crew would go back out to the raft towards evening and get the lights going where someone would keep an eye on it throughout the night while the **Princess** would lay off drifting a few hundred yards away. We'd then wait for morning which made for a lazy afternoon especially for me. Time to work on my tan. At four a.m., everyone was back in high gear.

CHAPTER 7

BASKING SHARK

Saturday, February 9, 1985
(Slightly west of yesterday)

At dawn we set on "our" log again and got another four tons, which makes fifty from the same log in four sets. Had an hour-thirty-minute flight after that. Nothing spotted.

This afternoon we found someone else's beeper and proceeded to put our own on instead. I didn't ask any questions. They didn't use the side-scanning radar and just put out the light raft and so we will drift here until tomorrow morning to see if the newly acquired log produces anything. The word is that some boats are doing well two to three days west of here. Not sure if this will put us in the Solomon Islands.

I feel more relaxed about the flying as each day goes by that I get a few more flying hours in. Hopefully by the trip's end, I'll feel like a real tuna chopper pilot.

I've noticed that this type of fishing year around as opposed to a short burst like in Bristol Bay is much more relaxed. Certain jobs here get done at sea. Like today they painted the boom whereas in Alaska, we do everything possible at the dock.

I'm starting to get some color on my white body. Now if I could just get my weight under control. My head has to be in the right place first so until that happens, I'll have a hard time. Glad I'm here.

Sunday, February 10, 1985
(11:30 a.m.)

We have now been out a week just scratching here and there and have 125 tons. This morning's set proved to be the biggest yet with seventy-five tons. So, it sure paid to stop on someone else's log! Actually, that was a lost beeper we found yesterday as the batteries were dead and the antenna was broken, so it was fair game.

The daily routine doesn't seem to be firmly established but evenings are pretty much the same. Dinner bell at seven p.m., at which time we also have a movie. Watches have already started at six p.m. At nine-thirty or so, it's time for bed. Reading, listening to music on tapes, or stretching get fitted in there too. Morning starts at four a.m. if we are on a log. Breakfast is at seven a.m. otherwise. The guys stacking net only get to eat hit and miss if we made a morning set on a log or waited until afterwards. That could range from nine to ten or eleven as it was today. And now its noon and the lunch bell has rung too.

There were four sharks in the net this morning. Only four to five feet long but deadly. I was glad to see the guys put them back over the side alive. Although later on in our trip, I noticed a few had had their fins cut off. I guess for soup. Who ate it I haven't a clue because it was never served in the galley. While the guys seemed to handle the sharks rather delicately when putting them back in the water, that was not the case with other fish. But then the others tend to die more quickly. Lots of fish in general are wasted because StarKist only wants the tuna that are four pounds or larger, and they dock the boat two pounds for every one that's under that. The crew is ruthless in deciding. The red salmon we catch in Bristol Bay average five to six pounds, so I have a pretty good eye for that size fish. I made the mistake of challenging Noli one time, saying the fish he was about to throw over the side was at least five pounds. I took it from him and weighed it—a full five pounds. Noli refused to keep it and barely spoke to me for days. The crew was constantly pitching fish over the side, none of which would survive. Plus, there are lots of fish that got smashed as they went through the block that hauls in the net if they happened to have gotten gilled in the seine. Those too are wasted. Food for other creatures. It's nature's way.

Not all the unwanted fish went over the side. I noticed the Samoans every once in a while throw a few back on to the deck away from the net they were stacking. I hadn't a clue what they were but they had the shape of the bluegill and crappie I used to catch before my move to Alaska. As soon as deck cleanup was completed, one of the Samoans disappeared into the galley and came back with several fresh lemons and tabasco sauce. While most of the crew disappeared into the galley for their late lunch, the ones left behind were busy cleaning fish. A squeeze of lemon and some tabasco and down the hatch it went. Well, if they could eat raw fish, I wanted to try it as well and sat down on the deck amongst them. Before I knew it, I was gobbling it down raw just as they were and relishing it.

Monday, February 11, 1985
(North of Samoa)

Another set on the same log as yesterday. Seven tons or so. Flew in the early morning and got back just before a rain squall hit. Could have been bad landing in that. Shortly after we land, Avey spotted a log with his field glasses. The log already had a beeper on it which was supposed to not be working and so very shortly had one of the *Pacific Princess's* on it that was working. It will be our morning set. It was a rather laid-back day from then on.

My "job" was to get some more color on my white skin, so I went up to the helicopter pad in my bathing suit with suntan oil in hand. After thirty minutes on a side, I was burned. Sure wish a thermometer existed on the boat that I could get my hands on. It seemed eighty-five to ninety for sure.

The metal deck was terribly hot—too hot to touch. And so it goes. Life is very nice here. However, it would not be a good place if you wanted to be somewhere else. But, for now I'm glad I'm part of it all.

While the flying is getting more comfortable, the helicopter has not been responsible for a single set. Felante tells me not to worry. My time will come.

Tuesday, February 12, 1985
(Noonish, still going west)

Gained another hour yesterday. Flew two hours just before lunch. Our morning set produced ten tons. Quite a comedown from what they'd hoped for from the already tagged log Avey spied.

Today, another ship came into our area. Fifteen miles close at least but didn't get the name. That's the closest we've been to seeing anyone since we left port nine days ago now.

Circled our first breezer late this afternoon. Supper is down the tubes for the guys because they are committed to get the net back aboard no matter what. We have yet to see what it brings.

Avey and I saw a small tornado today (water spout). Gave it a wide berth as it was lifting water off the surface to over a thousand feet. Wouldn't want to get caught in one of those!

It was really exciting watching the whole operation of setting the net from the helicopter. A movie of it all would be fantastic! Seal bombs going off, green dye in the water, a speed boat dashing around inside the net at full bore to confuse the fish until the net was closed with Avey, the captain, screaming orders the whole time. I won't forget my earplugs the next time.

We landed when the net was closed. Lots and lots of sharks mixed up in the school of fish. Wouldn't have been a good place to have gone down for sure!

Anyway, it was a neat day (four hours of flying in all). Netted thirteen tons. Long way from the thirty to forty expected but a lot better than none.

Wednesday, February 13, 1985
(Still heading west)

Bad weather all day. Cut some ivory to keep busy. Thinking of making some bracelets. Also learned to make the monkey's fist knot from Noli who must be over the fish incident. I made three so far. Nice day. Also, we saw our first other boat this morning.

Thursday, February 14, 1985
(Valentine's Day)

Still heading west. Flew a couple of hours this morning. Saw a breezer right away and a log with a basking shark lazily swimming nearby. We "spiked" the log but the line broke on the beeper. When the *Princess* finally found it, it looked promising, so we waited out the night—light raft and all. After they'd set on the log and it was daylight enough, Avey and I set off again in the chopper, looking for more logs in the surrounding area without breakfast. It wasn't long before the report came in the fish weren't there. Avey was furious and was swearing into the mike. He ordered me to get him back on the boat. When we got there, I tried the normal approach to landing which meant I had to hover along with a tail wind. A no-no for sure! So, we approached from the port side of the *Princess* where I could face into the breeze—landing from the port side was another first. Macho and Mace were busy on the other side, keeping the *Princess* pulled off the net as it was finishing being pursed. When we finally landed, Avey told me to keep the engine running and showed up minutes later carrying his AR-15 and off we went again. This time in search of the shark he swore was stealing his fish. I could hardly believe my ears.

Basking sharks (the first I'd ever seen other than in photos) are gigantic. Sometimes more than thirty feet long with huge mouths three or more feet wide. They lazily swim along near the surface with their mouths agape (thus looking like they are basking in the sun) sifting out plankton they encounter while moving along. I suspect the entire world knows they don't eat other fish except, it seems, Avey. By making large circles it wasn't long before we spied it again. Avey wanted me to hover along, keeping pace with the shark a thousand feet below us but enough to the side so he could get a shot.

Taking his frustration out on a poor, defenseless creature didn't sit well with me but I did as he said; he was the captain. However, since I was the captain of the helicopter, I controlled that. As he stuck the rifle out his door and started firing, shell casings were bouncing and flying everywhere inside the bubble. What if one wedged down in one of the rudders? Did he even think of that? We would be hard pressed to get back on board the *Princess* without rudder control. He may have been the captain but I made sure the chopper moved ever so slightly from left to right and back again seemingly without moving any controls. The bullets striking the water below were scattered far and wide but I never could tell if he ever hit anything. Finally, he was out of ammo and miraculously the rudders still worked. Back to the boat.

CHAPTER 8

"HALF NET" SEAL BOMBS WASTED FISH

Friday, February 15, 1985
(7:30 a.m.)

We are on our morning log set. The one last night was termed a "shit set" as only one fish was caught. It's a big ocean even with a mile of net.

A huge marlin came on board this morning. I'm guessing it was pushing 600 pounds. I am supposed to get the spike, thus the term marlin spike, and all these years I thought it was invented by someone named Fred J. Marlin or something similar.

We got forty tons in the set. Before any word came over the intercom about warming it up, I looked over the chopper. Greased everything (except the tail rotor, which was hanging too far over the edge) and put lemon pledge on the bubble hoping to help the rain showers shed off easier.

In all I got about six hours of flying in this day. Located nothing but flew across the International Date Line (180 degrees W) into Saturday. When we got back to the boat it was Friday again. A first for me.

Saturday, February 16, 1985
(Heading southeast now)

Our morning set was a bust. Avey was not in the least happy. I did not get the marlin spike I was anticipating from yesterday. Evidently, we went flying too soon. Glad I managed to take photos.

My new schedule of not eating supper only lasted one day. Chiu has a terrific fish stew and I caved in. The movie the *Marx Brothers* did not do much for me so I left and read in my bunk and then fell asleep and then was awake from one a.m. on. Not a good policy. Will do better in the future.

Kind of a slow day. We (Ray J actually) repaired the throttle on the chopper. Will now have to relearn how to fly it! I also drilled some holes in my ivory for the bracelets I'm making. Finally flew about four p.m. I did manage to get my "skin cooking time" in. Getting some color now. Couldn't resist steak and baked potato at supper. Of course, this was after having fish at lunch with all the trimmings. Oh yes, our morning set produced zilch.

One thing I've been aware of, especially when flying, is how beautiful the rain showers are. They are isolated so you can see the entire shower at once. Flying close to them is another story as they have strong winds. Very strong! Hopefully I'll get some photos.

The stars at night are really neat. Almost wish I'd brought a star book along so I could learn more about the constellations. Father John is going to point out the Southern Cross one of these days, or should I say nights.

Sunday, February 17, 1985
(2 weeks out 6 a.m.)

We traveled all night to our "strange beeper" for which we've been looking for ages. Father John pointed out the Southern Cross to me at four-thirty a.m. Another first.

We are not too far from Fiji now (slightly north) and evidently in a forbidden area. No transponder allowed on in the helicopter because, obviously someone else could pick it up. Don't know how good our chances of being found would be if we went down as they can only see ten miles from the boat without it. Father John is somewhat concerned even though Avey doesn't seem to be, so that's something.

Was thinking yesterday when sitting up by the helicopter that the next time I go across Kansas or Nebraska or North Dakota, they won't be the flattest places I've ever been to anymore. The sea gives your eyes lots of room to roam and in fact there is a certain feeling of freedom here in that it leads to any place in the world. Probably a sailboat would give you more of a free feeling because fuel wouldn't be a problem. This little boat gobbles up 3,500 gallons each twenty-four hours. We had 180,000 gallons when we left the harbor.

We also had 8,000 gallons of fuel for the helicopter but the speed boats use some of that.

Monday, February 18, 1985
(Northeast of Fiji now)

We traveled all afternoon yesterday and all night to get back to this beeper this afternoon. Didn't make it in time for a pre-dinner set, so here we are drifting again with nothing to do. I "de-rusted" and painted the chopper jacks this a.m. and have just had my daily sun bath until a shower came along and drove me inside.

It was rather tough travelling yesterday with the rough weather. I felt a little queasy so had to lie down a couple of times. Spent all evening and night in the bunk. Did watch the movie *Silkwood* though. Pretty good even though I'd seen it before. No flying this day.

Tuesday, February 19, 1985
(International Date Line, 180 W 11 S)

Very busy afternoon flying. We spotted an "uncharted bank" and a couple of 200-ton foamers. Made a set on one of the foamers, which might have been perfect had Avey even thought to consider when Noli shouts out **"Half Net,"** that's what he means. If you're laying a circle and half the net is used, it seems rather obvious that it's time to use the other half of the net to complete the circle. But no, he's yelling to Father John, "Keep going, keep going, okay now turn," thinking the boat might head off and stop the fish. But those few seconds ultimately mean the two ends of the net will be a hundred or more yards apart when the net is completely laid out. Those lines and cables then need to be closed up before the fish escape, which leads to lots and lots of unneeded activity. That extra activity as I mentioned earlier, would make an exciting movie what with the bombs going off under the blue water laced with green dye. The circling speedboats churning up white foam as they made their tight turns in the greenish water adding still more drama.

I also used seal bombs on occasion in Bristol Bay to keep the harbor seals from ravaging the salmon in our gill nets. The bombs are partially filled with sand that make them sink and have a rather short fuse and would blow your fingers off if one happened to go off before you wanted, or would certainly do serious damage. The bombs are thrown as far as possible from the deck of the boat and make loud muffled sounds going off under the water. Avey always had me take the helicopter down near where the net was being closed so the thrashing of the rotor blades and the bumping of floats on the water would add to the confusion. With the speed boats making tight circles nearby, splashing water into the cockpit, and hundred-pound tuna sometimes bumping into your floats, you had your hands full. Especially if a cable surprises you coming up out of the water in front of you about that same time. It was a busy and dangerous place.

Avey was beside himself every time the fish escaped but everyone on board knew he was the one who ignored Noli's shouted **"HALF NET."**

Years before, a fish captain from another boat was lighting the bombs with his cigar and tossing them out the door with the box of seventy-two on the floor between his feet doing pretty much what we did when we were down close to the water. An ash fell off the captain's cigar and managed to light one of the bombs exploding the entire box, which killed both him and the pilot. Never did hear how the chopper fared but, needless to say, no more seal bombs are carried on board helicopters.

Now let's back up to the uncharted bank. A bank is an underwater volcanic mountain being formed at the ocean floor that hasn't risen above the water's surface. Think island and you will get the picture. Avey called his uncle as soon as we spotted the dark shadow beneath us. "Hey, Unk, is there a bank indicated on your chart where we are?"

"Nope. Nothing."

"Stand by. We're going to give you some measurements." At which point Avey had me make a big circle to line up with the longitudinal axis of the future island and cautioned me to make sure I held the speed at a constant sixty mph. Avey looked at his watch the instant we crossed the edge while I flew the length of the bank. He gave Father John the number when we got to the other edge and then we did the same for the cross section. "OK, Unk, mark it on the chart." Sixty miles per hour translating to a mile a minute is handy anywhere.

Avey, I later learned, had once set the *Princess* on a shallow bank when he was just learning to be the spotter and ruined a million-dollar net. Oh well, sons do make mistakes. Obviously, his dad forgave the blunder. Everybody makes mistakes.

Wednesday, February 20, 1985

Today is my daughter's birthday. Hoping to call her this weekend when the ham radio is up and working.

What does a fisherman do with a night off in the middle of the Pacific Ocean when the water happens to be only one hundred fifty feet deep? He goes fishing of course. With hand lines no less. I was awakened at five a.m. just to be able to see what the guys (who had stayed up all night) had caught and soon found myself with a line in hand. Didn't land anything but did get my line cut off once which was pretty exciting. I didn't plan on killing anything unless we were going to eat it. A lot of beautiful red snapper, barracuda, tuna (big, toothed ones) and some rock fish bit the dust for nothing it seems although Chiu did clean a barracuda.

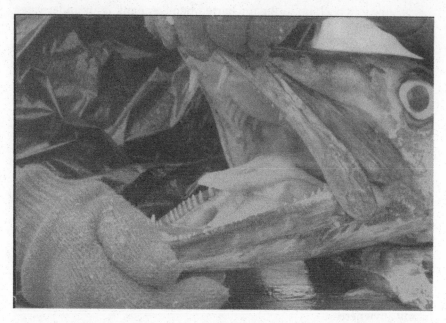

Seems everyone got sick out here once on bottom fish so now according to the Peruvians, they were all NO GOOD. The Samoans did not agree.

So what will the day bring? Who knows? Thought we were going to fly at dawn but evidently not. Made the mistake of bugging the captain about as to when—won't be doing that again. On my own boat I don't like being quizzed, so should have known better.

Tuesday, February 26, 1985
(At some point we crossed the date line)

It was a pretty big day yesterday with all the flying involved. Had a headache brewing all day. By supper time, I was in my bunk with a cold cloth over my eyes where I stayed until this morning.

The boys caught some squid last evening and we had some for lunch. Another first for me. A little tough and a bit too spicy but OK.

Avey came down with a cold so I got to fly with Father John in the morning and once again with Raymond Falante in the afternoon. Ray and I almost flew back to the wrong boat. Oh yes, we have been joined by Avey's cousin, Biscuit, on the boat *Louise V.* They seem to work back and forth a lot, exchanging information, etc.

We are now heading into a new area. We've seen a lot of fish here near the banks but most are small. Avey's cousin got ninety-five tons on his log this morning. We flew right past a small island and did so yesterday as well. Was hoping for a chance to land but no soap. Supposed to be forty people there and a radio a few years ago. Couldn't have been more than a couple of miles across in any direction. Wondered where they got their drinking water and what they ate. Sure would be a neat spot to visit.

I've started Samoan lessons with Masalino (Chiu's helper). He's very quiet spoken and mild mannered. Looking for someone to show me around Samoa when we get back. Maybe he's got a sister!

Also, I learned that Macho (whose real name is Labor Day because that's the day he was born) and Mace, his helper in the skiff, had been bank tellers in Pago Pago for several years before they decided to cash in on the source of the big checks their friends brought to the bank after each trip. They've now been on the boat for several years. Mace got married trip before last and now would rather stay home. Labor Day has plans for hanging on.

Near the date line
(8 degrees S)

Didn't see much activity flying today but the guys did spot a big log with the glasses, which will now be our morning set. Ray changed the oil in the chopper this afternoon and I helped.

Got a chance to talk a bit more with Labor Day this evening. Nice chap. His ultimate goal is to find a sponsor who will back him for a year so he could travel the body building circuit and see if he's got what it takes to win. He is the most muscular person I've ever been around so Macho fits just fine.

Already, my Samoan lessons with Masalino are not going well. Seems I'm pretty dense along those lines.

Saw another island but didn't get very close. Got sunburned by falling asleep past my prescribed time in the sun. Hoping to call Wisconsin tomorrow. We shall see.

Heard Chiu say at one point this afternoon that we are out of oranges.

Oh yes, I now know water swirls down the drain clockwise when you are south of the equator. Or, at least it did on the boat. I have since found out that there are many forces at work on such things besides the Coriolis force. Experiments carried out at the University of Sydney in Australia and MIT in the US have to be very carefully conducted for any consistency at all.

Was finally able to call my daughter over the ham radio on board but she was out gallivanting, so I got to talk with Penny, my former wife and still good friend. Using the ham radio to make a call isn't like picking up the phone and dialing. It makes for a very non-private call when every ham in the world is listening. Even with those concerns, I'd never before talked with anyone who was 7,000 miles away. Penny struggled with the "over" part so the ham operator knew when to switch a lever so the other of us could talk. But she was glad to finally hear something from me and knew Maria would be disappointed she didn't get to talk with her dad. I told Penny I'd try to call again near my birthday in March because that's when Maria was having her wisdom teeth pulled.

The movie last night, *The Marathon Man*, was quite a complicated and very brutal flick. It's amazing how each night that's what we look forward to—a couple hours of TV.

Our log set this morning went sour as a line broke on the skiff and they lost the rings on the net's bottom so could not purse up. Avey, of course, was livid. Later we tried to set on a school from the chopper but they outsmarted us and dove down. He wasn't happy about that either.

I made my best landing to date this morning. Good breeze blowing, which helps, but my technique was much smoother too.

We've been moving west all last night and all day too. Actually, it is now officially termed east because of the date line but the direction is still the same. And, technically it's also the next day but I decided I don't need to bother myself with such details just because we crossed a particular longitude.

We finally spotted a log (thanks to the boys in the mast) and stopped about two p.m. It will be our morning set.

Lifted weights with Macho the body builder and Mace this evening. Actually, I watched but they showed me some things for my back. I'm really stiff compared to Macho.

The movie was *Moby Dick*.

An interesting observation about going to sea: time stops. It wasn't until I talked with Penny that I realized the rest of the world goes on. Here, each day is basically the same. Night comes then morning but everything is still the same. The routine goes on. Look through the glasses, eat, fly the chopper, repair net, look through the glasses, eat, maintain watches, set the net, eat, exercise, putz with projects, read, sleep, watch the movie, practical jokes, work on something—anything just to keep busy. Day after day. Time stands still. Only the "dry" world keeps moving on.

Another observation: rough weather. Waves here need to be bigger just to fit into the surroundings. I'm sure the waves I've seen here are the largest in my life, yet they don't appear large probably because I'm on the largest floating platform I've seen big waves from.

Monday, February 25, 1985
(8 a.m.)

Our morning set has been going poorly. Lots and lots of small fish getting gilled. Really rough on the crew, not to mention Avey.

Tuesday, February 26, 1985

Finally, some fish! Our log set produced thirty-five tons. That's the good news. The bad news is we killed and threw over the side seventy-five to eighty tons because they were undersized.

It was very demoralizing for me, so I went back and helped sort fish. To my surprise, I found I wasn't welcomed. Andy finally took me aside. "Listen, Ted, we have lots of workers here but only one pilot. If you get wacked across the head with a chain or hurt in any way, we'd have to go back to port and find another pilot, which could easily add another month to this trip. Just stay out of there." Finally, because of all the messing around, even the good fish went bad and so everything was dumped. Such a waste! This was the cannery's fault directly, and in my mind totally immoral to kill and waste food when it is food that comes from the sea that it is owned equally by the world.

StarKist, as well as countless other processors, DO NOT have the authority to run havoc on world food supplies just because it costs them a fraction of a cent more to pack the smaller fish in a can and get it to market.

When you dock hardworking fishermen two pounds for every one pound of tuna under their four-pound limit, in my book is going over the line as well as immoral. I decided then and there I would do everything in my power to get that changed or at least put the ball in someone's court who could. I am ashamed of myself for never following through on my promise. It's not an excuse but John Lennon had it right: *"Life is what happens while you are busy making other plans."* Well, it's been thirty-eight years but now at least you know!

CHAPTER 9

"STORM CLOUDS" AND BIRTHDAYS

Rough weather is still with us. We found another log late this morning, so we are drifting again with a beeper on the log. It showed lots of fish—now how big will they be and how many will we waste.

Haven't flown in days it seems and I'm getting bored. Waiting really does take concentrated energy. A couple of things are bothering me out here at sea. Pollution is the big one. Everything not wanted goes over the side. That includes all garbage, waste motor oil, paint, and even fuel if need be. They carry about 40,000 gallons in the fish holds to start out and if they haven't burned it up when the hold is needed and can't find someone to take it off our hands—over it goes. Wonder why it is that man leaves trash wherever he goes? Land, sea, and now even outer space? Ultimately, man will have to live in his own shit. Why isn't that plain?

Ultimately, I forced myself to throw my first "trash" overboard or anywhere else for that matter. What came to me was that no matter how carefully I put an empty oil can into the trash, making sure the lid was securely refastened, someone would come around later and take the trash can to the stern and dump the contents into the ocean. The first oil can I tossed off the top deck, I watched floating until my eyes hurt and it was out of sight. Another first in my life but one I could easily have done without.

The other thing I've been pondering is the air-conditioning. We live out here in a make-believe world. When it gets too hot to be outside, it's easy to go inside. Chiu says that if the air-conditioning goes out, it is almost impossible to be anywhere on the boat sleeping or eating. As it is now, when I wake up in the morning, I sometimes dress with too many clothes on because it is so cool in our room only to go outside and find it sweltering. In the galley, where Chiu spends most of this time, I suspect air-conditioning isn't an option.

Thursday, February 28, 1985
(East of the Solomons, which are east of New Guinea)

I've been reading a guidebook about the islands in the South Pacific and enjoying it very much. Really interesting stuff.

We are still pushing on to the West. The bad weather (for fishing) is still with us and it seems to be with the whole fleet (based on what comes over the radio). So, we are not alone even though it seems so at times. We've only seen two other boats since leaving port twenty-five days ago.

Time now seems to blend in more and more into a single unit. Not days, not nights—just time.

Really have to get busy doing something now. You can only stay in your bunk so long. I've managed twelve hours each night now for a couple days' running. It's been too miserable to go up on the deck at night. While it's still eighty-five degrees, the wind and rain make it a poor place to pass the time. Saw our third boat today.

Friday, March 1, 1985
(N.E. of the Solomon Islands)

The poor weather is still with us although we did fly a couple of hours this morning only to have to land in a rainstorm. Avey and I saw it coming but before we could react, it was upon us. One second I knew which way I had to fly to get back to the boat and the next I hadn't a clue. My hunch was we had to go to the right. I asked Avey and he thought we should go left. I chose his way and for several anxious minutes, we slowly worked our way through the pouring rain, having to look out the doors to really see anything. Finally, there was an opening and the **Princess** was right before us. Avey had been right. What would have happened had I chosen to go to the right? That's as close as I ever want to be lost at sea—ever again!

Was up top a while ago trying to get a feel for the wind and guessing it was about thirty mph with at least one gust much higher. The waves are more like swells with some of the tops blowing over. In the book *Staying Alive*, they must have experienced all this although the man and his wife were in the water with a leaky rubber raft, which is about as close to the sea as you can get. They were finally rescued by a Korean fishing boat after 140 days floating around. Wonder if the Koreans were fishing tuna like us?

Started a macramé project covering a bottle yesterday but it got so rough I got a little woozy. Macramé is something I never thought in my entire life I'd waste my time doing but it was actually kind of fun.

Saturday, March 2, 1985
(300 miles north of the Santa Cruz Islands)

The above was according to the bridge. Certainly, a different Santa Cruz than the one I was familiar with.

It's official now—we are experiencing a storm at sea. Woke up this morning with the TV and VCR practically sliding off their table. Got out of bed but had to grab on to something to keep my balance at every step. Finally made it up to the wheelhouse and looked around. I'd never seen waves that big! We were not underway as I thought but were drifting in the trough. About a quarter mile away, another tuna boat was lying to in the trough as well. As we rode up the side of one wave, the other boat disappeared altogether. Now these are 220-foot long super seiners, three stories high with conning towers rising above that. For that much boat to disappear, the waves were huge!

I finally asked if we were in a hurricane and Father John, Avey, and Raymond F. all said at once, "***You don't ever want to see a hurricane. Period!***" Then Father John added, "We'd be running for our lives if it were. In hurricanes, the winds start at eighty and go up from there." I later learned you run because the waves in hurricanes are what they call "confused." You never know from which direction they will hit you and you could lose the boat. I guess not! I was already having enough trouble keeping my feet under me. In a way, though, it was pretty nice. Movies on TV, food with wet towels and blankets on the galley tables to keep things from sliding around too much and sleeping. But the waiting wears you down.

The one thing you quickly learn on a boat that is moving up and down with regularity is to take advantage of the weightlessness you feel on the down side of the swell. I sometimes could take four steps at a time when coming up from the workshop in the engine room by waiting until the boat was going down. Waiting for the boat to come up made it just as easy going down because you just wait for the steps to come up to you. Naturally there was no net mending happening on deck. But some things had to be done. Making sure the helicopter tie downs were secure and tying other things in place so they couldn't move around was about all I do.

When I looked over the edge today and down into water, it struck me that I was looking down two miles. WOW! Maybe there are organisms down there that thrive on mercury. Wouldn't that be something! We don't know anything about what's down there other than that's where all the garbage will end up after the Mariana Trench is full. The southern end of the trench continues nearly 500 miles southwest of Guam.

Exploring around this afternoon, I discovered a small bird inside the helicopter room. Keeping out of the weather it seemed. It flew out when I came near but went only a little way before landing on a line again. It did not appear to be a sea bird. Where had it come from this far out in the ocean? Maybe blown by the high winds and smart enough to find a place of shelter. Glad I could tiptoe away.

Planned on calling my daughter today but our ham radio antenna had blown down in the early a.m. Bent right over like a fishing pole with a big fish on the other end. That put a crimp on that!

Sunday, March 3, 1985

Still drifting although the wind and weather in general are getting better. The waiting is tough. Eat, sleep, read, watch TV, movies (Avey decides what and when), but it's a nice diversion.

Tried some shark fishing today. No bites.

The ham radio antenna got fixed but only Australia came in. I figured Penny wouldn't appreciate a collect call from there, so there was no calling my daughter.

Monday, March 4, 1985
(My 46th birthday)

We finally started moving again today. It's still plenty rough but it was good to start fishing. Unfortunately, the door flew off the chopper in the wind, which broke the plexiglass in several places. Father John got mad at me for it. One of the tie-shut lines broke—it was a shame it happened.

I baked my own birthday cake. It was a crazy cake and my favorite at the time. Also helped Chiu bake cookies. Kind of fun but tough to bake a cake when things are moving around so much.

Everyone wished me a Happy Birthday and Father John broke out the liquor stores so everyone could have a celebration drink. Even the teetotaler had one but couldn't finish it. So Macho finished mine and several more of his own.

He and I had another nice talk this afternoon. I may get to visit some of Samoa with him when we get back there. Today starts out our second month at sea.

Tuesday, March 5, 1985
(Same area)

It's three p.m. and it's been a nerve-wracking day all day long. Three sets so far and problems on everything, including the chopper. Ray just changed the alternator as the battery wouldn't keep the radio operating. It's time we started catching some fish!

Thursday, March 7, 1985
(Somewhere in the South Pacific Ocean)

The weather just doesn't seem to want to let up! Again it's cloudy and rainy with an occasional squall. Tried to work on the helicopter door this afternoon and got caught in a rain squall. Had the door off and was down stairs in the shop working on it but got soaked trying to get it back on.

We are still driving around the same general area. It is still plenty rough but at least the sun came out and I took a half-hour sun bath to celebrate.

Worked on the chopper's door most of the morning, stitching it together with stainless steel safety wire.

We put a beeper on a large log also so it would appear that we'll get to make a set tomorrow morning. What we need is to locate five or six logs and work them all and get this boat loaded.

Guess I was hoping we'd be on the downhill side of 1,100 tons by now but here we are still trudging uphill. Oh well, that's the way it is with fishing.

Pretty good movie this evening even though I can't remember the title. At least we got to see it to the end. Stretched up on the deck and that is feeling better all the time.

Still eating too much. Wish the weather would slack off a bit but, on the whole, life on the boat is OK.

Friday, March 8, 1985

Finally! Our dry spell of ten days without a fish has been broken. The log we set on this morning produced fifteen tons and it seems we are going to set on it again tomorrow as well.

Started up the chopper this afternoon only to find one mag was a bit rough. Avey said no, so we tied it back down. Ray has it off right now.

The rain squalls and wind are still here, although I got an hour in the sun about noon and managed to burn my face. Not too smart.

Seemed to be a lot of problems during the set this morning. The log (a very large one) got entangled in the net and several guys had to go in the water to free it up. Falante told me later he about crapped his pants when a whitetip shark, as long as he was, swam right under him. He scrambled for the corks in a hurry. The tow boat was in danger of swamping continuously and the brailing net broke as well, so Avey wasn't too happy even with some fish.

I've noticed changes now that we are into our second month at sea. Of course, it could be the fishless spell we've just come through but the Samoans are definitely on a "slow down." No doubt because of the way Avey talks to them (always cussing them out when things go wrong). Father John, who started out a bit standoffish is now unbearable all the time. Even Falante (Father's buddy) has mentioned it. Noli, who started befriending me again after the fish weighing incident, has become sullen towards me.

Anyway, it isn't pleasant in the galley during meals when Father John and Avey are there. Andy tends to goad them a bit and I don't have a clue what that is all about, so stay clear of it. I decided I don't have to be part of any of these games and so try to conduct myself like all is OK. Like at breakfast when the entire crew waits out in the hallway until Avey is finished. I decided to use **LIFESPRING** (a personal growth training experience I had years before) that teaches you don't have to let other people's problems become your own. Just click your heels together and move on.

I'd just walk past all the guys in the hall and go in the galley and sit down right beside Avey and in a pleasant voice ask, "Well, how you doing this morning, Av?" He'd come back with a bunch of mumbled grumbles and I'd just drop it and go ahead and eat my breakfast.

Later, when I had the chopper warmed up and he arrived and climbed in, I'd say, "How you feeling now?" Again, the grumbles.

Mentally, I clicked my heels together. He was not going to spoil my South Pacific cruise. His problems were his own, not mine.

But I do feel sorry for the guys when Avey starts belittling them. It got so bad I knew I could not fly the helicopter if I was being treated that way but Avey has always treated me with respect. It sure would be a tough situation if that ever changes as I'm really sensitive to things like that and that's why my heart goes out to the guys even though I'm sure Avey doesn't really mean it. Maybe someday I'll get to fly for a captain who, like a good football coach, can get the team on his side one hundred percent. That would really be fun! Of course, there is always the possibility of getting someone worse.

Saturday, March 9, 1985
(Noonish, basically same area)

Started out a very fine day. Weather was down with a huge spot of fish to boot. The chopper wouldn't start, the skiff's shaft went out and we missed all the fish except one shark. Avey was beside himself. And then it started to rain. Heavy shower after shower.

We are starting our sixth week right now. The first three went rather nicely. The past three have had some problems. Hopefully Avey won't always take out his frustrations on the crew (and he has had cause for plenty). As friend Jack Dean once told me during a week's stint on my boat: ***"Heavy is the head that wears the crown."***

We definitely need to find some logs and begin loading down the boat or at least start nailing some of those schools we've been setting on and missing.

We don't have all the problems, however. A boat in the tuna fleet (***Toro Bravo***) sunk this morning. Not many details yet. The crew all got off okay. It was an older boat.

It was a nerve-wracking day for everyone. A person can only tolerate so much yelling and cussing but the unfortunate thing is, the guy getting hurt the most is the guy doing all the screaming. Hopefully he will catch on soon to the truth that we all make our own worlds.

P.S. Avey finally met with everyone in the galley after supper and in his own way tried to apologize (in two languages no less as some of the Peruvians still struggle with English). I think everyone really appreciated the effort.

It was more a pep talk and a reassurance that when he tells someone to do something—do it! He has a reason but he is open for better ways and since he is the captain, that's the way it should be. Don't know about the crew but I felt better.

CHAPTER 10

GUARDIAN ANGELS

Monday, March 11, 1985

Bad weather again this morning. Wind thirty-eight mph top deck. Avey wanted to set in the worst way as a "foamer" kept tempting us all day. Finally, he gave up and we started steaming for parts unknown. The rumor is we are headed back to our last log.

Another boat (three days north) caught 300 tons in their net but lost it when the net ripped open. A shame as the fish were probably about spent crowded up like that and either dead or wouldn't make it.

Did some work on the chopper (painted the jacks and "sewed" some more on the sliders for the door). Worked on and finally finished another of the ivory bracelets I've been working on. Got a nap in too.

In the evening, I went swimming with the guys in one of the fish holds that was filled with water for ballast. Never swam in a pool where you had to worry about a surge. Here if you didn't get under water at the right time, you chanced getting your head bashed against the ceiling.

Unless we run into a string of good luck, we are looking at a three-month trip. Ugh! I, of course, was hoping for seven weeks as this boat has been known to have done often. Obviously, Murphy is alive and well.

Sort of miss not having more communication out here though. But maybe that's a good thing for me for a change.

Last week we were out of laundry soap. And Chiu said today: "No more fresh vegetables next week. Only a dozen apples left."

The chopper on the **Louise V** went down today. Evidently tail rotor failure.

I probably shouldn't be writing this when I'm upset but feel I must. Avey is either having a nervous breakdown or is simply crazy. His yelling and screaming are going to get us all in trouble. I really thought after his little pep talk the other evening he was going to calm down a bit. He wasn't thirty seconds in the "stick" this morning when it all started over again, only seemingly worse.

I feel that if we have to go in to any port for any reason, I'm going to get off the boat. I can't stand being around such things. What that would mean down the road career wise—I don't know. Avey has treated me very fairly so far so I really don't have any reason personally for wanting to do this but my gut is trying to tell me something. I would do it for sure if Falante got off. The other guys are married to the boat. I don't know—hopefully it will all work out.

Seems the latest "on board drama" is a war between Avey, the captain, and Andy, the chief engineer. We sure have enough troubles without more but I can see both viewpoints. Avey is being a bit childish, but he is the captain.

Another chopper went down today from **Sea Gem**. It was a Hughes 500C. The bird was recovered.

Also, for some reason, I suddenly feel OK about all the turmoil on board here. Earlier I was upset—especially a couple days ago with what happened in the mast. But now I am quite calm about it. Still dread a confrontation but even that's easing.

Wednesday, March 13, 1985
(Northwest of yesterday)

Finally flew again. That part was okay but problems still plague us. The seine skiff's rudder broke when it slid down into the water. That wasn't too bad until late in the day when they spotted a small school. "Very small," said Falante. This time the skiff's transmission was full of water. And to top it off, they set (actually Avey set) us in a riptide and everyone was in lots of danger from things happening with the net. What did they catch? Thirty fish! Falante estimated it to cover the bottom of the brailer.

Oh yes—everyone else was at fault.

Friday, March 15, 1985
(4 p.m.)

We went across the equator sometime during the night. Wish I'd gotten up to do the drain experiment right on the equator. Maybe on the return.

Rumor is we are headed towards the "pack." Lots of boats and fish supposedly. Sure hope there's at least fish. Flew two flights today (four hours in all). Falante and I went up this morning and Avey and I just now. Not much activity but Avey and I did see a very nice swordfish lazily swimming along on the surface obviously enjoying himself. Didn't have my camera. Ray and I saw lots of porpoise on our flight. On a later flight, Avey and I spotted a giant manta ray doing pretty much the same thing as was the swordfish. From a thousand feet it looked twenty feet or more across. I later learned the world record that was actually caught had measured thirty feet wing tip to wing tip. Had we actually seen a new world record? And while I had my camera, Avey saw no reason to waste time to go down and take a photo.

The weather has taken a fantastic turn for the better. They say it's because we are above the equator and away from the cyclone area. It's not quite glass but it sure is smooth with very gentle swells. Very pleasant!

Noticed considerable difference in my taking off today. Much more power needed. Landing too! Going to try it with the boat under full power to see if the extra breeze helps.

Andy got my message out to his wife today. She is going to call the Golles' and hopefully they will call Penny. Would have liked to talk with Maria via the "ham patch" as it would have been a good experience for her.

Also, we had a seawater party today. Drank my first water from the onboard water machine. A reverse osmosis thing under 800 psi. It shouldn't be possible but it was and I WAS THERE!

Saturday, March 16, 1985
(Still going westerly)

Big flying day. Four flights—nearly eight hours. Unfortunately, no fish. One set and it was a blank.

Saw another boat today. The **Jean.** We are still headed towards the "Pack." On one of our flights, we spotted the largest whale I'd ever seen. Was it actually the largest animal on earth—a blue whale? Wish I could have gone down for a closer look. The sea was smooth again.

It seems we all get lessons in humility when we least want them. I'd been feeling pretty good about my flying again. Takeoffs and landings were becoming routine. I think it's because I finally got a chance to fly the way I remember. Up and down on the logs over and over again. You get a good feel for the throttle and everything started to come back. At least I hoped so and I loved it.

Whatever possessed me to attempt to adjust my landing on the little red T in the circle on this day evades me still. Next thing I knew the **Pacific Princess** drove out from under us just like I'd been warned it would and the tail rotor was all of a sudden back amongst the twenty-six antennas. I couldn't believe things were not already disintegrating but instinctively cranked on full power and pushed the nose forward, which gave the tail rotor some clearance. Avey and I were both looking straight down at the deck.

Back on the cyclic again, which put the tail rotor a second time amongst the antennas in the stern.

Avey by this time had unhooked his seat belt and was hanging out the door looking back screaming, "You're going to kill us! You're going to kill us!"

I couldn't believe we missed the antennas again. This time I pushed the cyclic towards the port side and now we were looking straight down into the water thirty feet below. The helicopter was parallel to the side of the boat and very close. I knew the tail rotor was going to catch the top edge as we plunged down towards the ocean but just before we were to hit, the chopper picked up the air it needed and we flew away entirely unscathed.

Back around to the starboard side and I set it down perfectly over the red circle. Avey was out of the chopper in a flash. Filipo was there with the chains to tie us down as I went through the cooling off and shutting down procedures, which take a few minutes. I then went directly down to Avey's apartment and knocked on his door. When he answered, I thanked him for not grabbing the controls because I'm sure we both would have died had he done that. He was rather noncommittal in his reply but I sensed insurance was involved. I couldn't help but notice he had completely changed his clothes.

Certainly, our guardian angels had been there for the both of us and it's the only reason I have to this day for me to be able to be writing this now.

CHAPTER 11

THE UGLY PRINCESS

Sunday, March 17, 1985

I've had the feeling lately that I was part of a pack of wild dogs stalking the Serengeti Plain of Africa. Our fishing fleet operates in a similar manner, except that our efforts are self-centered in that each of us keeps the prey it kills rather than sharing it. However, the hunt is the same. We wander back and forth, always knowing where the others are and how they are faring. Continually sniffing out hotspots and then converging on it as the pack scrambles for bits and pieces of the prey.

The ocean was flat calm for as far as the eye could see. No relief anywhere except in the clouds and a few squalls.

We are below the equator once again. Went north-northwest and now southwest. Another full day in the air. Four flights. Nearly eight hours again. No fish although we did see two whales and one sea turtle. Another set of dry sets today. The guys are tired!

We are seeing more and more boats as we get closer to the pack. Avey actually sees them as he has the binocs, although we did fly over the *Sea Wolf* this evening. We are supposed to exchange some parts with them in the morning. Supposedly there are Koreans, Japanese, Slavs, and, of course, Americans in this area. One purpose only—tuna. I have the feeling we are the only ones wasting it, however.

Have heard that enough has been caught and killed and then dumped to have sent us home twice. I would guess they will hunt these oceans until they produce no more. Then where will man be? I hope we find a log tomorrow. Need to break out of our string of bad luck.

Monday, March 18, 1985
(North of New Guinea)

Another exciting day! We start to see logs. Lots and lots of logs. Too many to count. And boats. Seven of our own group plus a half dozen Japanese boats. All chasing tuna. We finally tagged a couple of logs and even made another skunk set but Avey was happy at least that he found a foamer on a log. Lots of flying. Eight plus hours, at least.

We could see islands to the north—the Admiralty Islands (near Papua New Guinea). Got a few photos from the chopper. Avey even let me get some photos of a really neat foamer with a huge sperm whale feeding amidst the tuna. It was like a movie in real life but in slow motion. The whale would come up through the foamer with its mouth wide open, spilling tuna out both sides. I was thrilled to be there watching the whole thing. The *Princess* was too far away for Avey to try to set on them or I'm sure he would have tried.

The present tach time on the chopper is 2363.2.

Tuesday, March 19, 1985
(The Admiralty Islands)

Busy day again! The weather has been absolutely beautiful (just like it's supposed to be in the south seas). Four flights, seven plus hours.

Not much on our morning set (two tons), except that I finally got the spike off a huge blue marlin. Why I decided to stick my hand and then my entire arm down its throat to see what it had been eating, I'll never know. What I soon learned was that pulling my arm back out was another matter entirely. They have tiny sharp teeth all sloping down towards the stomach (which I couldn't quite reach even with my entire arm extended up to my shoulder). Pulling my arm back out inflicted so many scratches they were impossible to count. Smeared the entire arm with antiseptic and toughed it out. Won't be doing that ever again! We tagged many logs. Hopefully some of those will produce our much-needed tonnage.

With all the boats, there is a lot of helicopter traffic. Have to keep a sharp lookout everywhere now. It was neat seeing the foreign boats setting this morning.

It was also neat getting so close to the beach when we were flying. I could distinguish coconuts on the palm trees. I wanted to go over and land to see if we could find a conk shell in the worst way but Avey vetoed that. "I don't want to get a poison dart in my neck," he said. I'd read stories about the headhunters that still roamed the jungles in this part of the world but I still wanted to go.

We watched the movie *The World According to Garp* the other night. Would like to see it again. Had Robin Williams in it. Very good.

Wednesday, March 20, 1985
(6:45 p.m.)

Heading northeast, I think. Our "big log set" turned up a hundred tons. Unfortunately, only fifteen tons of that was four pounds or better so eighty-five tons went back in the ocean—dead! What a crime!

Only one flight today. This morning while they were still brailing, Avey had me fly over to the *Louise V* and land on their deck. Their helicopter was sitting on the front deck in pieces. Wish I could have checked it out closer and talked with the pilot but Avey had me keep the chopper running so I was stuck.

Later, we saw a pod of whales, eight or nine in all. Got some photos but not very good ones. Didn't see any fish to speak of and after landing back on the *Princess* and the guys had finished the set, we picked up our remaining beepers and headed out of the area. The area that was to load us in five days.

We are still not even half loaded. Hopefully, we'll get into a slug of tuna here soon and turn this whole thing around.

The weather turned rainy this afternoon. It has been spectacular for a week or so now.

It's now 10 pm. We are drifting beside another log for the night. The light raft is glowing brightly a few hundred yards away. The movie is long over. I stretched a bit and then had to go blow it by having ice cream.

What I find going on right now in my mind out here is that time is blending together more and more. First individual days started melding together and now weeks are fading together. As far as the "beach" is concerned, time is frozen to a standstill. No references out here to keep one tuned to daily events. No newspapers; radios and TV always blasting away at one's senses. Just the sun and the night. Work is almost always the same and I find myself looking forward more and more to seven p.m. when the dinner bell rings and the workday ends. I don't have to stand watches.

Since there is a TV in our room and the VCR is working again, thanks to Andy, we can watch it without all the noise in the galley. While I'm usually alone, tonight the two Rays, and Andy came in and we all chopped up the James Bond flick we watched and talked about lots of different things. Actually, a very pleasant evening.

Still there is a certain urgency to get the boat loaded and head in even though it is somewhat relaxed.

Thursday, March 21, 1985
(3:30 p.m., heading southeast now)

We've evidently pulled up stakes (beepers) and are heading for new territory. Our morning set produced one fish literally. Couple of flights so far. Expect some more.

Big news is that I got to talk with Penny this afternoon. She had not gotten my earlier messages via the connections in San Diego so has been a long time wondering. Tough talking via the radio when you are not used to it and she was not very communicative. Perhaps she feels the "nakedness" of talking on the old-fashioned party line where instead of a few neighbors listening in, it's the entire world. Can't blame her because I feel it too. Guess I'll find out when I get back. Wish I'd remembered to tell her about New Guinea. I don't want a poison dart in my neck either.

We need some fish. Tons of fish! The sooner, the better for me but all fish from the sea are gifts of the gods. We'll just have to be patient. What else can we do?

Friday, March 22, 1985
(Almost 6 p.m.)

A very easy day. Started off by not catching any of the sixty tons of fish the sonar spotted on our log this morning. A huge disappointment to more than just Avey.

But things took a turn for the better. We went to our BIG LOG they elected not to set on yesterday because it was right on the bottom (uncharted no less). Today it was off. Actually, it was on fish yesterday and not the bottom as they thought. Hopefully, the fish will still be there tomorrow.

So what did I do all day since there was no flying? Almost nothing. I did carve out a couple of ivory rings and read a *LIFE Magazine* with some interesting stuff in it. Sunbathed on the top deck and finally went swimming with the guys after jumping into the ocean from the helipad (nearly three stories high). Pretty exciting when all anyone talks about are the sharks hanging around the boat. Managed to lay up on the top deck and watched the clouds but find I tend to close my eyes and daydream a lot when I probably should be more present in the here and now.

Falante and I talked some more about what working on a boat is worth. Ten grand minimum for selling this much of your soul and perhaps more! He's getting paid $15,000 as a "paper carrier" (Master's papers for a

250,000-ton vessel) which qualifies him as navigator but he could just as well be running the entire boat as does Father John.

I'm quite sure I spent as much effort and money getting my commercial helicopter's license as Ray did his Master's papers. Even though pilots don't do a lot of work, each time the helicopter leaves the deck, the money becomes immaterial for the risk involved. How can you put a value on life? Similarly, on a ship or any seagoing vessel, your life belongs to that vessel until the end of the trip and that portion is gone forever! Everyone has to personally confront the question of what we do with the life we were given.

Saturday, March 23, 1985
(7 p.m., heading easterly)

Another disaster day. A big net roll-up that took the better part of the day to straighten out. From our early morning set at twilight until nearly one p.m. The fish that were on the log yesterday were not on it this morning.

No flying again. Busied myself with some Ivory; then helped Chiu in the galley for lunch. The guys were exhausted.

And so we continue on. Tomorrow will be the beginning of our eighth week at sea. For the past two years this boat has not made a trip longer than seven weeks. To date, we have a demoralizing 400 tons on board.

Sunday, March 24, 1985
(Still heading easterly)

Because it is now one-thirty p.m., the time we left the Pago Pago dock, our eighth week has officially started. We have been running since yesterday afternoon. Destination? Unknown at this point.

No flying again. Rain showers most of the day. I'm feeling a little down. Managed to keep busy most of the time until now. Ray J, Andy, and I did sneak a peek at *Butch Cassidy and the Sundance Kid* at some point. I napped for a couple of hours and sharpened my Buck knife. A Real Big Day! But, I should enjoy it. It's a nice lazy time in my life. I may never have it this good again but I have to laugh because I've always had it good.

We could see islands all day in our travelling. They should be the Solomons.

Monday, March 25, 1985
(Near the Solomons)

Some real excitement this morning. Seems we set on someone else's beeper at five a.m. Who's going to know? Right! A skiff was launched almost immediately to drag the log with the beeper attached as far away as possible, just in case. The crew was busy pursing and brailing when we spotted black smoke on the horizon. Obviously, we're not the only tuna boat equipped with radar. The black smoke got closer and finally we could see the boat itself. Steaming full bore right at us! I was on the top deck by the chopper so had the best view. As the boat got closer, it slowed to a near crawl and came right up along our starboard side. It was the *Nippon Maria* (a Japanese seiner very much like ours but without a helicopter). Every hand on board lined their port rail with their clenched fists in the air above their heads. Even their chef was out there threatening us with his meat cleaver. It seemed every set of eyes was staring holes right through me. If I could have crawled under the rubber mat on the deck, I would have done so in a second. I don't think I've ever been more ashamed of anything in my life. Here we are representing the United States of America and acting like ghetto hoods. Stealing the fish from a damaged, out of commission beeper still attached to a log is one thing. This was outright theft. I'd never been exposed to anything like that in my life. From Avey's point of view I'm sure, since they were Orientals, who cares? Well, obviously I did and everyone on board the *Nippon Marie* certainly did. I seriously doubt the Japanese, who, I've heard, wash down the slime from their decks and then somehow save it to later make into artificial crab meat, don't throw any tuna away regardless of the size. We Americans, on the other hand, waste more fish than we process and even resort to thievery.

Eventually the shaking fists disappeared over the horizon. And while I was embarrassed to have them see me on the top deck like they did, it was even more painful to come upon them again later in the day.

By now Avey and I were in the air, doing our regular thing when we came upon a group of boats hovering around an obvious breezer. The *Nippon Marie* was at the center of the whole thing. Avey called his uncle, "Get to where we are as soon as you can."

The *Nippon Marie* was obviously timing the rising and falling of a Breezer so as to set their net accordingly. I made wide counterclockwise circles around the entire group so Avey wouldn't have to take his eyes off what was happening. I could hear his curses getting more and more riled all the time. "Black smoke it, Unk!"

"Almost there." We made another wide circle and could see the *Princess's* black smoke. "Come to where we're hovering," which Avey had me do once we saw the *Princess.* When Father John finally eased up behind us, Avey was screaming at the Japanese but it was only me and the bridge on the *Princess* who could hear his rants. He wanted them to set and set NOW! Everyone in the crowd of boats who was watching knew the protocol and was patiently waiting a turn. I wondered how many countries they represented? The boat finding the fish had full rights to the first set. Avey knew the protocol as well as anyone but next thing I hear is him screaming at Father John, "Screw it, Unk; get ready to set." Seconds later, he screamed, "Let it go! Let it go!" Dutifully, the *Princess* obeyed and poured the coals to it.

The Japanese were obviously watching and almost immediately dropped their skiff and net and steamed full bore right across the *Princess's* bow. My insides were screaming "YES! YES," while Avey was screaming a barrage of cussing aimed at the *Nippon Marie.* The Japanese were not going to get the set they were calculating for, but they were under no circumstances going to let the *Pacific Princess* make off with a second batch of their fish the same day. Father John had no choice but to slam it into reverse under full power or risk having the Japanese seine wrapped tightly around our propeller.

What were we telling the world about Americans? I certainly didn't feel any pride to be one at that moment and here it was the second time I felt that way in the same day.

I couldn't help but wonder how many countries were watching the "*Ugly Princess*" in operation.

CHAPTER 12

FUEL

Tuesday, March 26, 1985
(Still near the Solomons)

A relatively neat day. No fish on our log set this morning but we did manage to snag a loose school to the tune of nearly seventy tons and so pumped up the spirit on board the boat. Later in the afternoon, we were not so lucky as that school gave us the slip.

We were sure needing a big day and almost had it, if only Avey learned to set the net end to end instead of having 300 yards of lines to deal with before closing the net. I can't say it isn't exciting flying down near the surface with all that is happening. After all I came for the flying as much as anything but loading the boat is what we need to get done and the sooner the better. Three other boats working in the area plus the Japanese.

We had visitors from the *Sea Hawk* today so I had to fly our bird off the deck so their bird could land. I was just about ready to take off when Noli crawled in beside me. That's when I learned the crew had never been for a ride in the chopper. I could hardly believe it and made a mental note to talk with Avey about changing that.

Wednesday, March 27, 1985

52,000 gallons! "What?" cried Avey.

"That's all the fuel we have left," said Andy.

We made another skunk set. Avey seemed ticked off all day. Actually, afternoon now that I think of it.

Pleasant evening up on the helipad.

Thursday, March 28, 1985
(7:30 a.m., same area)

Twilight on our morning set. "What do you see on the sonar, Ray?"

"Nothing, just a couple of scratches."

"LET IT GO," says Avey. And so we continue our daily pattern.

Everybody else has it figured out that the fish around here are return- ing to the logs later in the morning so they don't show up on the sonar until later. You just have to be patient. Patience is obviously not one of our captain's virtues.

And, of course, there is the big log that had solid markings from ten fathoms to fifty fathoms that we left a few days ago. No one has that one figured out yet!

No stretching tonight. Two movies instead.

Friday, March 29, 1985
(11:30 p.m., north of the Solomons)

Another absolutely beautiful, almost-slick, calm day. Of course, our beloved leader caught us no fish once again but perhaps it wasn't his fault. Perhaps that's just the way things are. I did fly three times and we marked a few logs. Hopefully, we'll start clicking on them one of these days.

"In a week, we'll be out of eggs!" says Chiu. In two days, we'll have been out at sea for two months. With 600 more tons, we will be going home.

It will probably be a long time before I climb aboard another boat going out to sea and yet I'm glad I'm here. Strange.

Saturday, March 30, 1985
(10:30 a.m.)

Another beautiful day. Our morning set was "shit" nothing. Where to now? Who knows? Greased the helicopter this morning and took some more weights off the tail rotor. Hopefully it will improve the pressure I have to keep on it to track straight.

Finally got to fly about five p.m. Missed the school. A darn nice one too and a good time to set. The tail rotor seemed fine. Landed practically in the dark.

Sunday, March 31, 1985
(9 a.m., still same area)

We flew off this morning at six-fifteen, probably hoping to catch the same school napping. Well, we found them and set on them but they weren't napping. So here we are at sea for two months and only half loaded.

Tomorrow is April Fools' Day. Sure would like to get Andy on something.

Things wouldn't be so bad if we had some prospects in sight but unless those in charge know something I do not—we don't. Only my faith which I still feel will top us off very quickly just as soon as we get past the 500-ton mark. We are officially at 495!

My back has been giving me some scares. Every once in a while, it wants to give way but doesn't. If I stretch it out in the evenings it seems to do OK but now with the private TV/VCR, I've been letting the stretching slide more often than I should.

Had an official breakfast this morning. Can't say I feel any better. Will go back to dried fruit tomorrow. Hopefully, by then we will be on the short side of a load.

Well, we do not make it to 500 tons plus in March. It's six p.m. and the chopper is buttoned down for the night. We saw fish earlier but couldn't set on them as a rainstorm was coming and we were nearly out of gas.

Really strange how cold a person can get when it's so warm here. I got wet covering the helicopter in the rain and before I could get to our room, I was chilled and miserable. Sure was nice to step into a hot shower. Ha! My civilized side comes out again.

The guys are all hoping for some fish soon. You can see it in their expressions mostly. Today our one set was technically very good, except the fish got out. We also circled a whale and it stayed quite a while with the speedboats circling outside the net. But, when it decided to go, BAM! Right through the net just under the cork line with one slap of its tail. This is a net made of nylon rope. A dozen men pulling on it in opposite directions couldn't begin to snap a single strand and yet with one smack of its tail, the whale went right through. It was impressive! Of course, the hole it made will have to be patched, but just as impressive was how small the hole was for such an animal. Even if the whale hadn't left so soon, we wouldn't have caught any fish because the net was still a long way from being pursed closed.

Monday, April 1, 1985
(April Fools' Day, 8 p.m., same fishing area)

The screaming of the hydraulics goes on and on. I find I wear ear plugs much of the time. In the chopper of course, now when the net is being pursed, and in the engine room below. I don't see how the guys on the net pile haven't gone deaf.

One-thirty p.m. Missed another good school with another technically perfect set and so the captain decided to vacate the area. Headed southwest the last time I looked. I've been busying myself working on some more ivory. Can't believe how grateful I've been to Andy for the use of his workshop as well as the material he gave me to keep me busy.

Tension is high on the boat. A fight broke out on the net pile while they were stacking this morning. Between Reuben and Filipo but maybe from an old disagreement. Anyway, the galley is like a morgue. Only a few guys go in there when Avey is there. Most try to wait until the coast is clear. I personally feel more uncomfortable when Father John is in there for some reason, although it is not good when Avey is there for sure! It would really be nice if we all didn't feel we were walking on eggshells all the time. Falante said that when his dad ran a boat, he was in the galley playing checkers with the guys and having a good time. That's how it should be here. But even the cook is afraid to ring the dinner bell when dinner is ready. Avey has to say, "Ring the bell," and sometimes that doesn't happen until an hour after everything is ready.

Tuesday, April 2, 1985
(North of the equator again traveling northwest, 7 p.m.)

As a reminder, Pago Pago is fourteen degrees S.

A very beautiful day at sea. Perhaps the calmest day we've had the entire trip. Absolutely slick calm. Had two flights today with Falante. Saw a whale and a few birds.

I'm again very unsettled about staying on the boat. This time because I'm jittery about Alaska and my fishing business up there. If we haven't caught any more fish and actually go in to Guam, I'm going to get off. If we get fuel (which I believe we are committed to do before very long) then the boat could stay out until June, which would be a disaster for me. There is plenty of concern about me getting paid if I do leave but all I can do is be as honest with them as I can be. But I must make that decision soon and get on with it.

Wednesday, April 3, 1985
(7 a.m., still a bit above the equator and still going northwest)

No stretching last evening and my back is hurting this morning. Probably my nerves. Another beautiful day but there is a big ocean swell. Unlike yesterday, when it was slick flat calm. We jogged all night.

I've decided I will not be able to go past Guam. But at this point, I don't even know the boat is going there yet. I won't do anything until we are actually there.

Eleven p.m. A big day in all. Four flights, lots of fish, and a set at five p.m. that netted us eighty-five tons. We are finally on the downhill side of filling the boat.

A beautiful full moon tonight. Too bad I'm too tired to sit out on the deck to enjoy it.

Thursday, April 4, 1985
(Near the equator, Sand Bank area)

A very busy day to say the least. The "wolf pack" caught up with us during the night. There were five boats around us when I woke up this morning. No doubt Avey couldn't refrain from bragging about our luck yesterday and so we have company today.

Lots of fish in the area but we end up not making a set. Lots of flying (four flights). Very nice, calm seas.

Friday, April 5, 1985
(Good Friday, north of Sand Bank)

Well, today there are ten boats around us. We traveled all night to get here and even the Korean boat that was around us yesterday was here this morning. Lots and lots of fish schools in the area. Some guys connect more than once. We strike out twice. Really stupid too. The guys are all down in the dumps. Can't blame them.

Five flights today (not all two hours but still long). Worrying about the other choppers is more strenuous than I realized. At least four in the air at times.

Again, the seas were very calm. A couple of times we hovered so close to foamers the smell of fish was strong in the helicopter.

Our sets were so bad I was almost ashamed of the *Pacific Princess*. You can't catch fish if the net doesn't get closed quickly. It would sure be nice to get this thing loaded before going to Guam, which I guess is mandatory now.

Talked a lot last evening with Falante about when I should spill the beans about getting off in Guam but he felt it would be in everyone's best interest to wait right now. We're in a good fish area and Avey just might blow up and fire me and then everyone would suffer with no chopper right now.

Ten-thirty p.m. After much mud-slinging in the galley (after our morgue-like supper), the feeling is the trip could go four months. I sure hope not! But we are dealing with an egomaniac for a captain.

Hopefully, he will luck out and circle a couple hundred tons and get us over the hump but personally I wish we would head for Guam. And there you have it—*another day in Paradise*.

Saturday, April 6, 1985
(North of New Guinea, same area as yesterday)

It's almost noon. I've been up flying twice already and we made our first skunk set of the day. Still lots of fish around but very difficult to stop.

Here on this side of the date line, the world is celebrating Easter Sunday (at least Christians are). I'm still tuned to Wisconsin time and of course know that Penny and Maria won't be going to Easter sunrise service until tomorrow. I already had one Easter sunrise as we were flying by six-fifteen a.m. This way, God willing, I'll get to have two of them.

The weather has been picture-perfect. The sea is like a smooth lake. Zero wind and hot as blazes. I just tried a half hour of nude sun bathing and couldn't make it. The metal roof was just too hot through my beach towel.

Hopefully I'll be able to concentrate on more of the positive aspects of this adventure even though I'm convinced the negative stuff will continue. I feel more and more every day that I will have to think long and hard before I put my life in someone else's hands ever again with no way to reverse the agreement. I am more than ready to take charge of my own life once again even though this has been a good experience for me. Probably should entitle this chapter "Time Stops but the Sea Goes On."

Nine p.m. I flew until dark and beyond (six-thirty or so). Another skunk set but one boat (the **Ferman**) managed to snag a school of 400 tons. Only trouble is that they eventually lost it in the sac. Another 400 tons dead without anyone benefitting. Sort of wonder if the ego thing isn't part of all this. "Ha, ha, I caught more than you!"

Sunday, April 7, 1985
(Easter Sunday)

Well, I've spent Easter in lots of places now. From Pennsylvania to Wisconsin to Mt. McKinley (presently Denali) and now here in the South Pacific.

Another beautiful day and to make it even better, we snagged a hundred tons this afternoon. Missed the second set this evening. Lots and lots of flying again.

Got to talk some more with Chiu today. He really did have it tough as a child. From being carried on his parents' backs to get out of China and being hungry until he was twelve when the American churches got involved. Then it was a big pot of boiled rice doled out one scoop to each person for the entire day. Not unlike the soup kitchens of our Great Depression. Everything happened through the churches, so if you wanted to eat, you attended church.

He said, "Kids today grow up too easy."

We can all be thankful that's for sure. Kids in the U.S. have never known war but I'm sure a lot more than we realize go to bed hungry.

Anyway, it was always interesting talking with Chiu. His father, now dead, retired a general in the Army.

Then to hear Avey degrade Orientals like he does when they are out here trying to make a living, just as we are, makes me wonder what we Americans are doing for international relations. They certainly must already have a poor regard for those of us on the *Pacific Princess*.

Well, the tonnage on board is now 650. A few more days like this and I can relax. But we were lucky today. What we need are logs! Can't help but thank the Lord for all small mercies.

Monday, April 8, 1985
(Same area)

The rumor that we are supposed to be getting some fuel from another boat out here at sea is no longer a rumor. It happened late this afternoon. Certainly, going in to Guam will now be postponed. Maybe we'll get the boat loaded and I'll be home free because there won't be any reason for me getting off at Guam if we are loaded and on our way home. Just hope we get it loaded by next weekend!

We got 20,000 gallons. Chucky, from the boat *Cherique II* supplied it. Lots and lots of activity as guys are visiting back and forth, obviously knowing each other. Fueling while safely tied up to the dock is one thing; fueling at sea is another matter entirely. Boats at sea depend on the space around them to keep them safe. When two 250,000-ton vessels narrow the distance to yards, everyone is on alert. Throwing a weighted monkey's fist attached to a light line from one boat to the other is the first step. That light line pulls a heavier one and the heavier one pulls the fuel hose from the providing boat to the receiving boat. Both seine skiffs are in the water tugging on their bow and stern lines much as when pursing the net on their respective seiners to keep the boats from coming together, but also not hard enough to put pressure on the fuel line connecting the two boats. Things are "humming" when fuel is being transferred. Besides the fuel line watchers and getting information to the seine skiffs, outboard skiffs visit back and forth. Extra food leaves one boat to resupply the other. Maybe tools or spare parts or medicine or VCR tapes get exchanged as well. It's like a block party at sea.

Tuesday, April 9, 1985
(Still in the same area)

It's now early afternoon. We flew several flights this morning but couldn't get the fish to cooperate. Chucky, however, managed to catch two schools this morning. I doubt it was all luck.

So now we are taking on even more fuel from *Cherique II*. I didn't really want that to happen the first time because I had visions of throwing in the towel at Guam and here we are doing it again so it must be right! Chucky is full and heading home. I feel we are going to load up soon and everything will work out fine. WE WILL LOAD UP SOON!

Wednesday, April 10, 1985
(Moved only a little east-southeast from yesterday)

The guys had a difficult night last night. On our last set, the net got a "roll up" (webbing wrapped around the cork line) and they worked at getting it unwrapped until two a.m. or so. And then back up at five this morning and on it again.

Had three flights today but no fish. A pretty nice day weather wise. Got some time in the sun, plus a nap.

Avey said he'd get his dad to get a message to Penny and Maria. Sure hope so. It's been too long without contact with "my circle."

The other thing was the "wolf pack" split up today. The fish were not there anymore so slowly they headed to the parts unknown (at least to me). At one point this morning, there were seven helicopters flying around the one remaining school. That's about the time everyone pulled out. We shall see what tomorrow brings.

The other interesting thing this evening was the flick. It was another porno but Ray, Andy, and I went to our room and watched *Miracle on 34th Street* instead. Still a great movie!

Friday, April 12, 1985

We are now offshore near the Admiralty Islands and can actually see them from the helipad.

The last few days have produced some fish. All of a sudden, our total on board is 810 tons. A 200-ton set would put us in "Fat City!"

This has been a rather strange day. Started off at twilight with our morning log set where we caught absolutely nothing—not even a single fish.

A beautiful day though as we head for one of our other beepers only to find it had come together in a tide rip with a second of our beepers and about a "million" other logs. The crew set about sorting everything out. Avey and I left to see what we could find.

About nine miles east, all by itself, we find another log. Check it out by hovering close over it to see what baitfish it held and it showed some half-decent sign. So Avey calls his uncle to have him plot us and the log on the chart and we keep going east but do not dye mark the log and of course save our own beeper for logs further away. We do not spot another log during our entire flight (twenty-nine miles out at one point).

Finally, we get back to the boat. Macho has my camera and is taking photos of us when we land (something I've wanted to get the whole trip). He actually took pictures before and during the departure as well.

Still, all seems OK. We (the boat) are heading towards our new found log. I catch some time in the sun and then go down to take a shower. But for some reason the boat stops. We do not go near the log Avey and I found at the beginning of our flight. Instead of checking it out with the sonar as was normal, one of the guys spotted it with the glasses and finds no birds (I find out later). But to not check it out with the sonar seems very weird.

I went to bed and slept solidly for three hours (two to five pm). So did Ray. Everyone is down again. The urge to sleep must be what our bodies do to us when tension is high.

Poor Chiu. Avey just came around to ring the dinner bell. It's six-thirty p.m. and he hasn't rung it for weeks before seven-thirty p.m. Tonight, we're having BBQ chicken and the charcoal was slow in starting and now he wants to eat an hour sooner!

It's a nice evening up here on the deck where I've started my stretching instead of down on the wet deck. I can now touch my head to my knees. Quite an accomplishment since last fall when I first got into stretching at all. My back is feeling better too although it does still hurt in the mornings. Due mostly, I suspect, to the worst mattress I've ever had the occasion to sleep on.

Glad this day is finished!

CHAPTER 13

NOTE IN THE BOTTLE

Saturday, April 13, 1985
(Near the Admiralty Islands at the west end of New Guinea)

It's 11 a.m. and I find I'm a bit frustrated this morning as I'm working on my last bit of ivory. Sort of my "worry rock," if you will. Even Ray J was down. We are all highly aware that the same old shit keeps happening over and over.

Avey shouts ,"What do you see, Falante?

"Nothing."

"Reuben, what do you see?"

"Nothing."

"Let it go!"

What did we get? You guessed it.

What seems to have come to me through all of this is that my life is flying by. One day I'm going to wake up and there it will be—all gone. I've really had a good shot at it so far and can only hope that something good comes of all the turmoil I've experienced here on the boat. Good for everyone. A noble thought? An example? Who knows? Perhaps one day it will all be clear to me. Until then, I will continue to follow my hunches, attractions, or my bliss if you will. What else can I do? Listen to your heart Ted! It will lead the way. I sure have a hard time listening sometimes.

It's now 11 p.m. I finally got to fly after lunch. We found lots of schools of fish (too small) and a couple of logs, which we tagged and then eventually abandoned after the boat traveled thirty-five miles to check them out.

P.S. Thirty-five miles out is as far as we've been away from the boat in the chopper. It would be a lifetime away if you were in the water waiting for the boat to find you.

Don't have a clue what the latest plan is. We are however, under way to the North. We need 200 tons!

Got to see the movie *The Right Stuff* again tonight. Guess we've seen everything now.

An interesting piece of information got to me today. Avey was overheard talking with his dad on the radio about the pilot. "How's that pilot doing?" he asked Avey.

"Okay, Dad. Lots better now than when he started." Or something to that effect.

I do feel a lot more relaxed now about the flying and the chopper in general but then we've had flat calm weather for a month. Perhaps though it was the feel for everything finally coming back. I don't mean for the mechanics of flying but a feeling of being one with the machine. Of course, I now have a lot more experience working the logs and hovering on the schools of fish, which earlier I was not able to get. That helped to bring the feeling back as much as anything.

Sunday, April 14, 1985
(Traveling north from New Guinea)

It was absolutely slick calm this morning when Falante and I flew. I did a practice autorotation down to near the water. And later did an actual hovering autorotation right into the ocean. Basically, to show him how dangerous it can be when you can't actually tell where the surface of the water is. Later, when Father John and I flew, I could do nothing.

It is official. We have an unloading date of April twenty-ninth. That's encouraging but probably meaningless, unless we catch another couple hundred tons this week and pick up our fuel from the boat heading from Guam to meet us. Our trip there is now officially canceled. We will still have eight to ten days back to Samoa so there are lots of "ifs" hanging in the air. By then I will almost be committed to head straight back to Alaska and abandon my Ford van stored at Golles' in San Diego. Can't really do much about anything out here.

Probably that's the reason men go to sea and always have. Zero responsibilities out here. Eat, sleep, and work seven days a week, week in and week out, month after month. You get to port, go wild for a couple of weeks, spend all your money, and then are back out to sea where all your needs are taken care of until you hit port again.

Chiu got upset with Falante over how Ray asked for ice cream in the galley. Could be the tension mounting again or it could be something else. Wish we'd get some fish and head home!

Monday, April 15, 1985
(New area, wind blowing)

Started seeing other boats today. "Polers," the kind that fish with rods and lines. They throw baitfish into the water to keep the tuna close at hand. The boats we saw were Japanese. I can still remember the movie starring Anthony Quinn I saw as a kid. Three men were working in unison with their three lines from their poles coming together to a single line with a big barbless fly. All three would sling the fly over their head and into the water and immediately snag on to a tuna. It would then take all three of them to jerk the tuna out of the water and over their heads onto the deck behind where the fish would almost immediately fall off the hook. And then the whole operation would repeat itself. This would happen over and over again until either the fish were all caught or perhaps the men collapsed in exhaustion. Three men meant a 150-pound tuna or a "three poler" as 150-pound tuna are still called today. A person working alone caught one polers. Two men, two polers, and so on. I can't believe I actually got to see the real thing.

Well, another day spent trying to catch the elusive school fish with two worthless sets. Avey, I found out later, had belittled the crew so badly they were all ready to quit. Except the Peruvians cannot quit—they have nothing to go back to. Actually, what upset everyone so much (I get all the details from Macho) was that Avey was broadcasting all his frustrations to the world via another boat or helicopter. The way the headsets are set up, I cannot hear who Avey is talking to when we are flying except the **Princess**. Evidently, they almost missed the log because Avey was so busy ranting and raving.

We finally ended up tagging two logs, the second of which I was almost embarrassed to be a part of the tagging. A Japanese boat had pulled up beside the log and was just sitting there. Avey sent me down to hover over it. It did show sharks and fair bait. So we proceeded to put a beeper on it right in front of the Japanese boat maybe a hundred yards off. Back we went to the **Princess** where Avey then immediately sends me back to the log with Felante to protect it. "*From what?*" I wondered.

That gave me five flights for the day. Seems like I was up and down all day. Anyway, I was tired by night with a bit of a headache. I must absorb more tension than I realize even though I don't actually feel it when it's happening.

There you have it. Another big fishing day in the South Pacific. I'll be glad when I get some control over my life again but I also wonder if we ever really have any control. Perhaps I just want to get on with my own thing.

It will really be interesting this week. I can only hope that Avey lucks out and hits a 200-ton jackpot somewhere.

I seem to be talking more and more with Macho. It's sort of nice. He seeks me out. Even Andy does at times. Falante has seemed to go into a hole or something. Short-tempered is not the proper term but "short" in other ways. Communications in general are very limited.

The strain is showing everywhere.

Tuesday, April 16, 1985
(Traveling north again)

No fish on our log this morning. A big disappointment to all. One flight this morning. We saw a beautiful reef, which had some fish but way too shallow for us. I guess we are on our way to rendezvous with the boat coming from Guam but we just stopped and exchanged something with *Sea Encounter*.

Fuel again is the big story onboard. We are back down to 43,000 gallons, which is basically enough for the trip back to Samoa. We are rumored to get another 15,000 gallons from the Guam boat. If all this is so, we have only the fuel to catch our remaining tonnage and then will have to turn for home no matter what. Of course, things change here from moment to moment, so who knows? If we don't load up, the guys lose some bucks and of course Avey loses face with his peers. Don't know what his dad will think.

One thing I haven't remembered to mention is that we had a minor accident on board a week or so ago and a sick case. Maniomie got clubbed on the head with a net ring out on the net pile and got quite a black eye and a cut. It's all healed now and his scar will be minimal.

Tony, one of the Samoans, came down with gout in his feet nearly three weeks ago and is still not walking. He crawls to the galley on his hands and knees. It's evidently an inflammation of the joints and very painful, somewhat like rheumatism or arthritis and quite common to Samoans. There are pills for it but either the boat is out of their supply or Tony forgot to bring his (perhaps the *Sea Encounter* is bringing Tony some pills) If not, the fuel transfer is supposed to include pills for Tony.

Back to the fuel. We are over 3,000 miles from Samoa. Ten days at 330 miles per day is 3,300 miles. If we are to make our unloading date, we have to head back in three days (I for one will be disappointed in that. HA!). But, we'll have to wait and see what happens. I'll believe Samoa when I see it with my own eyes.

I'm getting very close to 200 hours of flying in the chopper so that's been a nice thing for me. I have really enjoyed flying again but I guess I like more leeway and freedom than I've had but still it has been okay. Next time (if I ever do this again), I'll do it in a Jet Ranger (manufactured by Bell Helicopter). I've finally found something I can do in January and February that is as exciting as fishing in Alaska. Not quite as profitable perhaps but potentially a nice thing to have in one's hip pocket to escape the cold and snow and the darkness of an Alaskan winter.

Wednesday, April 17, 1985
(South of Guam)

Fuel again! This will be our third block party. Also, we will get some food, which I hope includes fresh lettuce. I'm sure the crew is hoping for beer. And then there's the pills for Tony. This time it was the boat *Claire P* out of Guam. They have a Hughes 500 on board. The pilot and I exchanged waves. Kind of nice as we are of the same fraternity.

Well, now the big question remains—how long will we stay out? No one will venture a guess and there is plenty of reason why—Avey.

Of course, if we were to run into 200 tons tomorrow, that would pretty much solve the whole thing. Let's do just that!

Thursday, April 18, 1985
(Rain everywhere)

It's two-twenty p.m. The best rumor ever! We are supposed to make it to Pago Pago by the twenty-ninth. Orders direct from San Diego and the horse's mouth himself. "Beeline it home!" We are now trying to beat a steamer into Samoa. If we don't, the *Princess* will have a two-to-three-week wait to unload.

Tried to take a nap but find I am too keyed up inside to sleep. Lots of things to start winding down here on the boat. We will have ten days of running (twenty-four hours a day) before Samoa so there should be lots of time. Probably won't make any real decision about Alaska or California until I reach Hawaii, even though I believe getting my return ticket to Alaska is the smarter choice. All that will take care of itself. I do think I should spend a few days in Samoa to soak up some of their culture and visit where some of the guys on the boat live. It's not very often you get to know people from foreign countries and I should take advantage of that.

Finished my ivory workings yesterday and plan to give all of it away. Macho told me the guys are now calling me a Samoan name, which means, "he who works with his hands," but for the life of me, it's gone. A bummer! I should have written it down at the time because I took it as an honor.

This morning I made a set of five dice in the workshop and plan on teaching everyone my favorite game that was introduced to me years and years ago as "Oh Shit." It's much like Farkle but also called 10,000 much of the time. The dice ended up as one-inch cubes made from very dark wood and I even painted the dots white after barely touching them with a drill bit in the drill press so they stand out. Can't wait to show the guys the game but have to wait for the paint to dry first.

I wonder if I'll ever get to fly the chopper again. I never really got to say goodbye to it properly but I will. It would have been better knowing it was my last flight when I was actually flying but maybe not.

At this point, I'm quite glad I stuck the trip out instead of bailing like I had the urge to do several times. I never did and then what would I have done if I had? It's a long swim in any direction.

I was amazed at how quickly the rumor swept through the boat today. BAM! Everywhere at once. For sure, no one was saddened by it.

Friday, April 19, 1985
(Still heading SE Yea!)

We have been underway since yesterday. It is hard to imagine we still have 3,000 miles to go to get to Pago Pago. I then still have the 2,000 miles to get to Hawaii and then 2,000 more to get to the "lower 48" and still another 2,000 or so to get back to Palmer, unless I go straight to Alaska from Hawaii.

My dice game was instantly very popular. But only after the Peruvians calculated the glitches I'd made didn't really affect the way the dice rolled after all. When I made them, I'd laid the cubes all in a row and dimpled them with the drill press one dot on each of the five dice. I then turned each die ninety degrees from how it way laying and then dimpled two dots. Turned them again and dimpled three dots and so on. I then put the five and six dots on each end. It was the first time in my life I learned the dots are very critically placed. The one dot is opposite the six. The two is opposite the five, three opposite the four. The two numbers have to add up to seven. Well, the Peruvians knew a lot about gambling with dice before coming on the **Princess**. When they saw the misplaced dots, they instantly said, "No, no, no, no," and proceeded to roll each individual die a hundred times keeping track of what numbers came up with each roll. Ultimately, they gave their blessings and thoroughly enjoyed the game as much as everyone else.

When Avey spotted everyone messing with the dice, he ordered them all to get busy and the rest of the day was filled with work details. Since I'm not considered crew, I took a nap while they worked, sunbathed on the deck, worked on my marlin spike, and took photos of Father John's beard. Not necessarily in that order.

Got weighed again and found I'm pushing 200 pounds but decided to eat supper this evening, ice cream included. Chinese food with a salad is hard to resist. We haven't had salad in ages!

Noli gave me a very nice gift today. A swordfish spike made into a small splicing tool called a fid. Today fids are actually made from metal and used on wire rope but that was not the case when windjammers ruled the seas.

Also, Father John and I had a brief candid talk about his position here on the boat. He's in a tough spot!

Saturday, April 20, 1985

(4:30 p.m., still heading southeast)

Change of plans! Probably the zillionth time by now. *"Fill the boat. Don't beeline it in."*

So we are off to the northeast, helicopter and all. After an hour's flight, we were back on deck and a couple of hours after that the boat was back on course to Samoa. That was this morning. This afternoon I sunbathed a long time on the top deck. Really easy living now! Kind of nice to get back in the air again. Although I was amazed at how rusty I got in so little time.

The guys finished painting the bow. Looks very nice but they ran out of paint, so the rest won't get much.

It's also Filipo's birthday today. He's 26. A big cake is baked in the galley and is being decorated.

I also worked at sanding on my marlin spike. A really nice trophy from the trip. Maybe I'll actually try to scrimshaw on it. The latitude and longitude where we got it and maybe the date as well.

We've stopped for some reason. Wonder what the next change in plans will be?

Sunday, April 21, 1985

Bad weather is coming. Wind and rain over a large area to the northeast. I tied the cover on the chopper and put jacks under it. Also put extra ties on the blades.

Wish we knew what the plan was for sure. It appears we are headed for a beeper left on one of our earlier logs (thirty-five tons). But the way things have been going, anything could happen.

I showed Father John and Avey the message I found in a wine bottle while fishing in Alaska. It was in a hammer-and-sickle-embossed bottle, with a large CCCP embossed onto the bottle as well. It was from Russian fishermen. It was a message of peace to the world and one of my most trea-sured mementos! It took considerable effort, but this is the best translation I found.

Pacific Ocean 11 May 1980. Boat BMR. Nadezhdinsk.

We are Soviet crewmen. We are from the town of Kakhodka on Primoria (Bay Ocean).

We send a friendly greeting to whoever finds this bottle. We are interested in who finds this bottle and the letter and where they found it.

I don't know what to say about myself. We are working and living very well.

We don't want to fight anymore. We want to make peace for the whole world—no more fighting. We ask that all young people of all continents to work harder to make peace.

We ask that all people have sunshine in their hearts. Then there will be no more fighting.

Since it was sent out to all people of the world and I was the one who found it, I felt obligated to pass it on. I sent a copy to Jimmy Carter when he was President. Also, Billy Graham and Paul Harvey got copies. I figured those three could spread the message the farthest. I haven't a clue what Billy Graham or Paul Harvey did with it, but President Carter sent me a personal thank-you letter.

Both Father John and Avey were duly impressed. Father asked many questions about it and even suggested I put my own message overboard from here. And perhaps I should.

CHAPTER 14

HEADING HOME

We are fishing once more in earnest. Five flights, two sets, one log tagged and another 100 tons onboard. The only bad thing was we traveled west part of the day to get the fish. Samoa is the other way!

Greased the chopper and noted the tach now reads 2490.2. I've now flown over 200 hours on the trip. Even got to take a few photos.

The weather is still beautiful. We ended up near a group of islands. Very high and rugged looking. Got a photo or two but haven't yet figured out what they were called.

Whales today everywhere. Really spectacular! A nice day in all.

Monday, April 22, 1985
(Still heading southeast)

Another change—no fish this morning, so we are now beelining it to Samoa. Seven days and eighteen hours to go. Even got word to jack-up the helicopter, so I may have flown it for the last time. Of course, if we just happen to see fish towards Samoa and can still make our unloading date, I'm sure it will be in the air once more.

A very relaxed atmosphere once again on the boat. "Oh Shit" is still popular and I'm glad for that. As I was sunbathing on the deck today and everyone else was chipping paint,

I realized this just may be one of the easiest times in my life. A three-month South Pacific cruise isn't something most people get to do. Good food, flying a helicopter, and getting to know people I'd never meet otherwise. Not bad when you consider I'm being paid six to seven grand to do this (the extra $1,000 is my bonus, which is quite unsure). Also, I was not pushing snow and worrying about freezing to death for the worst part of an Alaskan winter. I only hope when it comes time to do this again, I remember the bad things.

Tuesday, April 23, 1985
(Still heading in)

It's 10:30 a.m. and already the trip home is getting long. Still six and a half days to go.

I finished my macramé bottle and tied another monkey's fist just to keep in practice. But it looks like I'm going to have to go chip paint to keep busy. It didn't bother me at first watching the guys working with paint chips stuck all over their sweaty bodies, because if they didn't want me down on the deck when they were stacking net, they surely didn't need my help now, but I was weakening. I did fix the door on the laundry room but it was only a minor job.

Wish I'd get some news that Avey's dad got through to Penny. It's been a long time since she has had any word of us.

Did a lot of thinking after the movie last evening when I went up to the chopper deck to do some stretches and watch the stars swaying back and forth. There were a few clouds, so straight up was the best view. Amazing the number of shooting stars there are in the southern hemisphere.

What came across was all the activities I've done in my life. And I've managed to do a lot over a wide range with this trip being right up near the top. But what it finally boiled down to was the thing that has given me the most satisfaction was the first story I ever got published. It was the best seventy-five dollars I've ever made—ever! To actually get paid for something that came out of my head still boggles my mind. Other things came up too. Building my flintlock rifle, the birch spoons I whittle and give away. Working with my hands—especially artistic things I love to do.

But even that first rejection letter I got has stayed vivid in my memory. It was from *Wisconsin Trails and Tales Magazine*. They were apologizing for not being able to publish the story I wrote about making maple syrup because they had already committed to another one but would be very interested in publishing it the following year if I would submit it again. Would I!

It is now nine-thirty p.m. We watched *Romancing the Stone* again tonight. Very entertaining but I guess I have a soft spot in my heart for anyone doing exciting things.

Got to talk with Penny this afternoon (evening in Wisconsin). Nice to hear a familiar voice. Not much news out of her except our daughter Maria made the Dean's List. Good on you, Maria!

Also, I went to work this afternoon scrubbing the shaft alley just to keep busy. Only five more days to go!

Spent a little time on deck this evening but the wind was too strong to really enjoy being there. Not rough, just wind. I suspect the boat moving along at nearly fourteen knots was part of it.

I'm supposed to be making bean waffles for tomorrow morning's breakfast. I tried to show Chiu about sourdough pancakes this morning but it's hard to explain leavening agents and the time factor involved. There's no leavening in bean waffles.

It looks and feels more and more as though I will go straight to Alaska from Samoa via Hawaii. Will have to call the Golles' and make sure they will be able to deal with my van I left there. A pretty nice day in all. The Peruvians had a great game of "Oh Shit" tonight. They seem to enjoy it a lot. They have played lots of craps in their lives. Wish I understood more Spanish.

Wednesday, April 24, 1985
(Written the next day, going southeast still)

Got up at four a.m. and made the bean waffles for the crew and to show Chiu how to make them. Father enjoyed them the most except for me, but Chiu did say they were very professional.

Turned into a headache day. Started off just fine but progressively got worse so I went to bed. Ended up vomiting almost to death. Ice bag, ice water, and finally 7-Up. After six hours, I was finally able to watch the movie.

Only worked on the shaft alley for an hour or so and managed to repair one of the galley chairs before the headache struck me down.

Thursday, April 25, 1985
(Still heading southeast)

I'm back in my "nest" after venturing out to breakfast (eggs and toasted bean waffles) because I still feel so beat up from yesterday's headache. I've been going to mention my nest ever since starting the trip. The bunks are oblong cubicles screened off by drapes so you can get a bit of privacy at times. They measure seven feet long and three and a half feet wide. A single mattress fills the bottom where in the old days they piled grass or straw or whatever they slept on. My mattress, quality wise, isn't much better. By morning I'm down in a hole, which I can barely roll out of—thus, the nest. But, it's cozy too. I have a headboard shelf and a book shelf a bit higher on the long side of the bunk. I have my tape player handy and earbuds, which make listening very pleasant and unobtrusive. Glad I brought another transformer so I don't have to depend on batteries.

It's going to be May before I can get to Alaska for sure, and it could easily be May before we get to Samoa, but I think they are still planning on the twenty-ninth. I could be gone the next day but feel I should spend a day or so taking in some of the atmosphere of a south sea paradise island— especially now that I know Macho and some of the guys who live there. It will mean so much more now. All that will have to take its own course. Will just have to wait and see.

4:30 p.m., ATTENTION! DO NOT MAKE ANY PERSONAL PLANS WHILE OUT ON A FISHING BOAT. We just got word that we have a five-day extension to try and get this thing loaded. Won't find out the details until later this evening but that order didn't come out of thin air.

Friday, April 26, 1985
(10:30 a.m., heading southeast again, went northeast for some time this morning)

We are back in the air looking for fish, and binoculars are everywhere. We had a small deviation in course to the northeast but now seem to be back on course for Samoa. Hopefully!

We saw no signs of fish anywhere on our little side tour but could still bump into a log with fish on it. Our problem right now is fuel.

30,000 gallons. Barely enough to reach Samoa plus a couple spare days so we shall see what happens.

I've noticed everyone is now edgy or moody. Avey especially. Can't blame anyone as we are all wanting this thing to end maybe for no other reason for some than to start out fresh on a new trip. Such is the life of a tuna fisherman.

I still marvel at how easy life has been for me on this first trip. No doubt I could have contributed more but always felt unwanted. Perhaps it was just me or maybe it was true what Andy said about only having one pilot but lots of workers.

It was very comfortable being in the chopper this morning. A far cry from my first flight away from the boat. But we are in even more danger now than back then as we have no electronics to help locate us should we go in the water. No radar, therefore no transponder and the Automatic Direction Finder is out of commission. That perhaps would be the most valuable as far as I'm concerned, but it has no cable and hasn't now for many flights. At least this morning I turned the beeper on before we left the deck. It only works about three miles out in the horizontal, which is how it is carried under the helicopter, but still better than bobbing around with nothing.

I also tried to keep Father informed as to where we were. Heading northeast off the bow, starboard beam, and so on. There was no accurate way to determine the distance without a stopwatch and the sixty miles per hour rule but at least a direction would help the boat find us for sure if need be. The chopper has been performing beautifully and I can only hope it continues for the rest of this trip and many others down the line.

Macho forgot to take the landing photos today. Hope I get another flight as those are some of the photos I have wanted for sure. I think photos looking down at the chopper in the process of landing would be cool. From coming over the edge of the deck to touchdown.

NOTE: We are traveling east now. Another change?

Flew two times today. Seems like we are only looking because we're supposed to. Not much life in our efforts from my point of view.

Still beautiful weather. Was up on the deck tonight watching the stars and saying goodbye to the Southern Cross. May not get to see this part of the world again. You never know.

Saturday, April 27, 1985
(East again)

And so the days pass. Things sort of blend together but not knowing when we are to go in doesn't help the spirit much. Perhaps morale would be a better word.

Eat breakfast, play some dice, check out the chopper, putz in our room, visit Andy's room and listen to the short-wave radio he now has in there and catch some world news. Lunch time. Dice, work on sharpening my knife, find something to read, take a nap, shower, get ready for supper. After the movie, a snack, more dice, up to the helipad to do some stretching, watch the stars (count the shooting ones) and enjoy the feel of the warm breeze. And finally, take a walk through the pilot house and crawl into bed. Another day at sea!

Sunday, April 28, 1985
(Heading south now)

Twelve-fifteen p.m. We have just started our thirteenth week at sea. Eighty-four days. Time to go home!

The weather has cleared somewhat. Perhaps it won't blow up after all. It is still cloudy though.

Eight-thirty p.m. Well, so much for me being a weatherman. It got rough. Nothing on our log, so we are going east to another one.

It's now 11 p.m. and another day has passed. A couple of pretty good movies tonight (*A Little Romance* and *For Love and Honor*). Both, for the second time. A dice game plus a baked potato and peach ice cream sundae and now in bed. We lost another hour of time today. Still, no one knows for sure when we are heading in but it surely can't be too much longer. It was a good day!

Bad weather is coming. Wind and rain over a large area to the northeast. I tied the cover on the chopper and put jacks under it. Also put extra ties on the blades.

I still have to talk with Avey about my bonus. I'd like that issue settled before going in so there is no question as to where I stand.

Monday, April 29, 1985
(Heading southeast again AND heading in!)

Six p.m. Avey's birthday (regret not asking his age).

Well, it is at least "semi-official." We are expected to get into Samoa at 10 a.m. Wednesday. Avey talked with his dad today and there is a chance we'll be on an airplane headed to Hawaii Wednesday evening (tickets are being sent).

My big concern has been my bonus ($1,000). So, I finally decided to hit Avey with it straight out. He said, after I asked him about it, that I did a hell of a job for him and he was well satisfied and that I could count on my bonus. He would even try and get me some tonnage to boot. That made me feel a lot better about everything.

And so tomorrow we are supposed to lay the net for cleaning—I'm to get to ride in the skiff with Macho and Mace. Looking forward to that.

Made a pig of myself on birthday cake and ice cream and couldn't sleep, so went up on the helipad to enjoy the stars and moon and the breeze. One of my last nights.

Monday, April 29, continued . . .

Somewhere along the line this day I managed to do my laundry and rounded up some of my stuff for packing, which I hope to do tomorrow. At least by tomorrow night. Lots of things to tie up between now and then: take photos of my projects, take photos of the Samoans in their lava lavas along with Ted in a borrowed one, note in the bottle to deal with (see below), take photos from the skiff if they set the net, record the tach time from the chopper, clean out my drawer and get organized, and finally prepare all my rolls of film for mailing from Samoa to the States if at all possible. Oh yes, I already cleaned the bathroom floor and shower as well as all the wood paneling in our room. Looked pretty good.

Note in the bottle:

I've done considerable pondering about putting my own note in a bottle and dropping it overboard like the one I found from the Russian fishermen, but for the life of me, I can't come up with anything even remotely profound as was theirs. Anyway, who would believe an arrogant American? Are we really that way? We must be because that's the way our boat has acted throughout the entire trip. I decided to put a copy of the Russian message in my bottle with an update of what happened and our current latitude and longitude at the time and let it go at that.

Thursday, April 30, 1985
(Going east, message in the bottle dropped)

We just finished making our last set where the net is laid out for cleaning, which finalizes the trip as far as fishing is concerned. This is where all the rotten bits and pieces of dead fish wash out as well as any other pieces of crud. While Falante spent most of his time in the wheelhouse, I noticed he was out on deck supervising the final covering of the big seine after it had been cleaned and restacked.

I got to ride in the skiff for the whole operation, including when they were holding the *Princess* off the net and even got a chance to go skinny-dipping. I quickly discovered how scary it was to dive into water a mile or more deep. Without exception, I turned up to the surface long before I got to the bottom of the dive worried I might not be able to hold my breath long enough to get back up. I even got to stay aboard when the big skiff was winched back on to the boat to its angled perch behind the net and the special keeper mechanism hammered closed to keep it there. A very enjoyable couple of hours.

Chiu paid me a rather nice compliment this morning. He had asked if I would be coming back on the next trip. I told him I had my own boat to go back to Alaska.

"We are going to miss you," said Chiu in much more broken English than that.

Then he said, "You more like writer than flyer. Helicopter no good. You speak like writer. Much better than fly."

And so we are getting close to our final day of travel. I am looking forward to getting back but really glad to have gotten to know these guys and to have been a part of all this. High adventure for me!

Wednesday, May 1, 1985
(Western Samoa is in sight)

The final day of my South Pacific cruise. Preparations are being made for landing at the fuel dock when we get in. We were again out of eggs. Everyone was up and about early. I was even up on the bridge at five-thirty a.m. to watch the dawn light. I said goodbye to the Southern Cross last night. Wonder if I'll ever see it again?

Avey and I talked this morning at breakfast about my pay. He is personally going to give me my $1,000 bonus in cash and see to it my final check is mailed to me in Alaska. Nothing about tonnage. Maybe his dad had different thoughts on that.

I am still wondering if I should stay behind a couple of days to see Samoa but can't really see myself getting involved in all the drunken celebrating that will have to go on first. I'll talk with Labor Day about it some more.

Nine-thirty a.m. Avey gave me my $1,000 cash. It would be pretty hard for them to try and beat me out of the rest now. Father says he expects we'll be at the dock at one-thirty p.m.

I managed to get some of the Samoan's names and addresses and decided I'd rent a car for the afternoon when we get in so I can see some of Samoa. Macho said he'd sneak away to show me around. That's when I learned the guys are expected to be on the boat during the day and only have evenings off.

Four hours to go! After three months, I'm now counting hours.

It's been hectic to say the least. Father John landed us almost to the minute he predicted. I expected to run down the gangplank and kiss the ground but no—at that point twelve official-looking Samoans (lava lavas and all) came marching up the plank. "Immigration," they announced.

They wanted all passports and for the entire crew to assemble in the galley. So, all nineteen of us, captain included, stood around while the twelve nonsmiling officials took seats at the tables their backs all lined up next to a wall and shuffled papers back and forth.

Finally, one of them said, "This is just routine (according to Avey, it was the first time) unless, of course, you have narcotics onboard."

"How could we?" whispered Andy behind me. "They were all used up."

It seems our captain had been known to indulge. And the Samoan crew had long ago smoked up everything they had brought. And there couldn't be much liquor left with all the birthdays celebrated on the trip. One guy even had five cases of beer delivered at sea to tide him over.

Some of the officials left the galley to go search the boat, leaving us all standing there like dorks. They wanted to check out the food stores and obviously look for drugs. Finally, they all got up and marched back down the gangplank. I swear one of the official's only job was to carry the stamping pad and their official stamp.

Father John then gives back the passports and issues strict orders for everyone to be back on board by eight a.m. sharp. Some guys head back to their room to pick up personal stuff, others get ready to take on fuel, and I get ready to leave to go rent a car so the Samoans can show me around the island.

The next thing I know Avey is yelling for the hydraulics to be turned on so the speedboats can be lowered. Believe it or not, he wants the rust cleaned off the outside of the hull before anyone leaves. Three months at sea, family waiting on the dock, and still they are trapped. WOW!

No rentals for half an hour, so I hoof it four blocks to the post office to mail my slides and make phone calls and then back to the boat to pick up my seabag before getting the car. I could hardly believe I had severe blisters on both my heels. So much for letting the motion of the boat do my walking for me.

After getting the rental, Filipo shows me the way to the village where I was introduced around as "Ted the pilot." Everyone seemed genuinely interested in meeting me. Kiso presented me with my own Samoan lava lava and a fine mat (le toga in Samoan). I could hardly believe it. Perhaps the most treasured thing in Samoan society and reserved for very special occasions. It can sometimes take six months to a year to weave one. Wow! I was impressed then and still treasure it to this day! Another of my life's high points. I even met some pretty Samoan girls and, of course, Kiso's mom. Tony (now walking again) made a special effort to show me the dice I'd made on the boat. Treasured enough to bring home to his village. I was honored once more.

I drank a beer with them all and then was off to the airport with Filipo as he wanted to take over the car when I finally boarded the plane. He'd return it to the rental agency tomorrow. The plane was late arriving but when it finally arrived, I got to meet Mr. Gonsolves himself. He personally gave us our tickets but no money exchanged hands. At least my bonus was in my pocket. Inside I'm not too worried so it must be OK.

And so at nine-thirty p.m., I'm at last on a plane Hawaii bound. Avey, Father John, Falante, Raymond J, and Reuben also boarded with me. I sat next to Reuben. A little while ago before I started updating my journal, I was lying back in my seat thinking: *Here I am sitting beside a Peruvian (Reuben is finally getting to go home to visit his folks after fourteen months), in a plane flying over ocean for nearly five hours, full of people from all nationalities of the Polynesian or South Pacific world. There is some kind of bond here among all of us. Especially between Reuben and me. I can see him zooming past me in the speedboat, throwing water up on the chopper as I hover dangerously close to the surface where tuna are swirling below. Both of us are fighting to keep the fish in the net just so we can load the boat and get out of there. Strange and yet nice in a way too. We don't talk much as my Spanish is nil and his English is hard to understand but we are the same. We have shared three months of our lives together at sea. Father, the two Rays, and Avey are here, too, but the closeness isn't there like it is here. The same feeling was there in the Samoan village. We had all just shared part of our lives together. All different people and yet all the same. I'm glad I went.*

They just announced that we'd be arriving in Honolulu at two-thirty a.m.

Thursday, May 2, 1985
(Honolulu)

We arrived right on schedule. Avey and the two Rays head for a hotel. Father John and I elect sit outside where we talked the rest of the night away. Reuben had to report to customs.

Father's tongue was rather loose. Seems they all had had plenty to drink. Avey was really bad. I was grateful I'd been in coach with Reuben. Father and I were together on and off until eight-thirty a.m. Most of what I had already formulated about the boat situation was confirmed including the fact that Avey needs some psychological help and, in fact, has been getting some except that it was forced on him. He, of course, doesn't see the need so not much is likely to come from it.

Father asked me to send him some photos. He was evidently glad I'd asked to take a photo of his beard before he shaved it off. I got the feeling he respected me and the flying, although on the boat it seemed otherwise. Just his way, I guess.

At some point I mentioned to him the Samoans had given me a fine mat when I visited them at their village. He could hardly believe it! "Do you realize what they gave you?"

"Yes, I think I do."

Fine mats are a treasure in Samoan society and at least one is treasured wherever I call home because it is always with me.

During the on-and off-times we had, I made some phone calls and managed to change my ticket from San Diego to Anchorage and even got a bit of a refund. Got back just in time to shake Father's hand before he boarded his plane to San Diego. Never did see Avey and the others. I still had time to kill, so I went and found a place to buy some tropical produce to take back to Alaska. Three cases of pineapples, two of papayas, two of macadamia nuts, and some mangos.

At five-thirty p.m., I was on board a jet and finally on my way back to Palmer. My great South Pacific adventure was now behind me.

EPILOGUE

When the plane landed in Anchorage, my good friend Kent Sandvik was there to meet me with my load of Hawaiian produce. It was 11:15 p.m. Fifty miles to the airport and fifty miles back home is a long trip. Since Kent had also taken me to the airport when I departed for California in January, I had left my Toyota Land Cruiser parked at his farm. But he thought it was way too late for me to drive the additional fifteen miles to the cabin I was living in at the time and insisted I stay the night.

It was strange to still have daylight when we drove out to Palmer because at the equator it would have been dark at six p.m.

We immediately cut into the mangos and pineapples when we got to his place and finally got to bed near two a.m.

Up early the next morning after having so little sleep and dressed up in my lava lava for Kent and Ibbie and friends Kert and Loraine Ukes who were visiting the Sandviks and had stayed overnight as well. Kert had once fished in Bristol Bay so I knew him well. I'd never before met Loraine. We had to jump start my Toyota to get it going but I had a grand time all day visiting and surprising friends in my bare feet and lava lava. I was standing in Arnold Witte's yard when he drove in from work that evening. Seeing a shirtless, darkly tanned, bare-footed man in a long skirt standing in your yard with piles of snow everywhere isn't something very often seen in Alaska. The look on Arnold's face was priceless.

Shortly after our fishing season that summer ended, I was back down in San Diego, where the Golles' (also freshly home from Bristol Bay) met me at the airport and took me home where I retrieved my camper van. There was no way I could thank them enough for taking care of my van for so long.

Also, while in San Diego, I tracked down Andy White, the engineer on the **Pacific Princess.** Andy was selective about the trips he took so fortunately was home when I visited. I met his wife Debbie and their two little kids. Andy was busy fabricating a radar support for a fancy yacht. It looked like it had come out of a factory. His reputation as a mechanical genius had spread and was sought out at every turn.

Next time I saw, Andy was in Sitka ten years later. By then I'd acquired a fifty-three-foot ketch rigged sailboat I planned to sail around the world. Andy was now the engineer on a very uppity sixty-five-foot yacht and had even brought his wife Debbie along for a trip to Alaska.

I asked him about the **Pacific Princess**. Seems Avey's troubles had finally caught up with him. Three years after our trip, Avey died of a drug overdose.